Organizing Logics, Nonprofit Management and Change

Nonprofit organizations are conventionally positioned as generators of social and cultural forms of capital for the common good. As such they occupy a different space from other types of organizations such as corporate firms that exist primarily to generate economic capital for private owners/shareholders.

Recent years, however, have seen professionalization promoted widely by funders, policy-makers and nonprofit practitioners across the globe. At the same time, there has been an increasing cross-over of employees from private and public bodies into nonprofits. But do such shifts open up space for the wholesale importation of managerialism into and commercialization of the nonprofit sphere? Are nonprofits at risk of being reconstituted as primarily economic entities, serving the interests of a leadership elite? How are such changes in an organization's trajectory brought about? What are the consequences for trustees, staff, members and the nature of managerial work? The authors engage with critical questions such as these through a unique insider account of one professional institute experiencing unprecedented changes that challenge its very reason for being. Drawing on a three-year ethnography, they narrate organizational inhabitants' struggles in their search for purpose and analyze the myriad of changes within different aspects of organizing including structure, strategizing, pay and reward, governance and leadership.

The book will enable readers to reframe and rethink organizational change as a process involving power, persuasion and authority, and will be of value to researchers, students, academics and practitioners interested in managerial work and organizational change in non-profit organizations.

Tracey M. Coule, PhD, is Professor of Nonprofit Work and Organization at Sheffield Hallam University.

Carole Bain, DBA, is Executive Education Fellow at the University of Sheffield Management School.

Routledge Studies in the Management of Voluntary and Non-Profit Organizations

Series Editor: Stephen P. Osborne
(University of Edinburgh, UK)

Voluntary and non-profit organizations are playing an increasingly significant role, worldwide, in the provision and management of public services. Drawing together significant and ground breaking research, this series will be essential reading for students of public policy and management as well as the thinking manager. Topics covered include the management of innovation and change, financial management, performance evaluation and management and organizational development and project management.

Also available from Routledge:

The Management of Non-Governmental Development Organizations
An Introduction
David Lewis

Financial Management in the Voluntary Sector
New Challenges
Paul Palmer and Adrian Randall

Strategic Management for Nonprofit Organizations
Roger Courtney

Regulating Charities: The Inside Story
Edited by Myles McGregor-Lowndes and Bob Wyatt

Philanthropy in Practice
Pragmatism and the Impact of Philanthropic Action
Ekkehard Thümler

Transformational Leadership and Not for Profits and Social Enterprises
Edited by Ken Wiltshire, Asatha Malhorta, and Micheal Axelsen

Organizing Logics, Nonprofit Management and Change
Rethinking Power, Persuasion and Authority
Tracey M. Coule and Carole Bain

Organizing Logics, Nonprofit Management and Change

Rethinking Power, Persuasion and Authority

Tracey M. Coule and Carole Bain

Routledge
Taylor & Francis Group
NEW YORK AND LONDON

First published 2021
by Routledge
605 Third Avenue, New York, NY 10158

and by Routledge
2 Park Square, Milton Park, Abingdon, Oxon, OX14 4RN

Routledge is an imprint of the Taylor & Francis Group, an informa business

Library of Congress Cataloging-in-Publication Data
Names: Coule, Tracey M., author. | Bain, Carole, 1969- author.
Title: Organizing logics, nonprofit management and change : rethinking power, persuasion and authority / Tracey M. Coule and Carole Bain. Description: 1 Edition. | New York : Routledge, 2021. | Series: Routledge studies in the management of voluntary and non-profit organizations | Includes bibliographical references and index.
Identifiers: LCCN 2020042119 (print) |
LCCN 2020042120 (ebook) | ISBN 9780367371005 (hardback) |
ISBN 9780429352676 (ebook)
Subjects: LCSH: Nonprofit organizations--Management. |
Leadership. | Organizational change.
Classification: LCC HD62.6 .C685 2021 (print) |
LCC HD62.6 (ebook) | DDC 658/.048--dc23
LC record available at https://lccn.loc.gov/2020042119
LC ebook record available at https://lccn.loc.gov/2020042120

ISBN: 978-0-367-37100-5 (hbk)
ISBN: 978-0-367-71104-7 (pbk)

Typeset in Sabon
by MPS Limited, Dehradun

To Susanne Tietze, a career-long mentor, the truest of colleagues, and the woman who inspired this book.

Tracey M. Coule

To Chris Gallagher, a former boss who set me on the path to post-graduate education; a valued friend and master "irritant to the [management] oyster" in the pursuance of good. As Harry Emerson Fosdick taught us,[1] the creation of a pearl is dependent on an irritation in the oyster's shell. Though the oyster does not like this ineradicable irritant, it is only due to its presence that the oyster gets the opportunity to do the most beautiful thing an oyster can ever do - make a pearl.

Carole Bain

1 Fosdick, H.E. (1965), quoted in C.L. Wallis (Ed.), *The Treasure Chest.* New York: Harper & Row.

Contents

Figures

Tables

Foreword

Angela M. Eikenberry PhD

What values guide our society and our living and working together, and who decides on these, are persistent political and governance questions. Today, the United States (my home country) and the United Kingdom (the setting for this book) are in the midst of struggles to define or redefine these values. U.S. Democratic presidential candidate Joe Biden's campaign has rallied around the slogan "we are in a battle for the soul of this nation," and a commenter in the *Independent* recently described the battle over Brexit as "a fight for the soul of the UK."[1] These conflicts over values do not just occur at the national level; they go on daily in the organizations in which we work, volunteer or participate. *Organizing Logics, Nonprofit Management and Change: Rethinking Power, Persuasion and Authority* is about the battle for the soul of an organization – in this case, a nonprofit professional institute undergoing changes that challenge its very reason for being.

In this engaging and highly readable book, Drs Tracey Coule and Carole Bain masterfully describe a struggle over two visions and realities of nonprofit organizational life: one guided by community logic and one by corporate logic. For better, or probably for worse, the authors illustrate how corporate logic, with its authoritarian and patriarchal tendencies, wins out, eroding the original community and charitable purposes of the organization. For those of us who want to keep our organizations democratic and focused on community and social benefit, understanding the mechanisms that erode these might help to keep them at bay.

Nonprofit organizations exist in a larger social context. Just as democrats and activists have been increasingly concerned with studying, understanding and challenging the rise of national authoritarianism and white supremacy, organizational practitioners and scholars are increasingly concerned with the pressures of managerialism and marketization that fundamentally challenge and change the democratic and social benefit roles of nonprofit organizations in society. I have spent nearly two decades raising concerns about the implications of managerialism and marketization on nonprofit organizations and on the democratic contributions they make to society. These include concerns about how managerialism and marketization affect a nonprofit organization's ability to create spaces for civic action and engagement; contribute public goods such as research, teaching, advocacy, or serving disadvantaged groups; and enact other important pro-social values. Many others have since brought to light similar concerns, but a large gap remains in understanding how managerialist and marketized processes come about and impact organizations over time.

This book fills this gap, providing an excellent primer to help practitioners and scholars understand how leaders can make changes to organizations – both small and large; obvious and obscure – over time to alter their very nature. Drs Coule and Bain draw on a three-year ethnography to illustrate the struggles and conflicts that occurred as a new CEO transformed different aspects of organizing, including changes to structure, strategy, pay and reward, and governance and leadership, to bring about an entirely new focus for the organization; one that often conflicted with the accountability expectations of its charitable status.

This work builds on more than a decade of noteworthy research by Dr Coule on organizing and managing work in nonprofit organizations and their linkages to wider societal arrangements, as well as Dr Bain's decade and a half of skilled administrative and reflexive practice in the organization under study. Together, they create a formidable team conveying a critical analysis that is truly enlightening, and that contributes to broader scholarship while being eminently practical. If you have ever worked in an organization where you felt a sense of unease or even angst that the organization's practices didn't seem to line up with the mission or purpose of the organization, or what the organization communicated to outside constituents did not coincide with what was communicated internally, this book is a must read. Drs Coule and Bain help us to see that what is at stake in such differences is about organizational values.

Carole Pateman argued in 1970 in *Participation and Democratic Theory* that organizational values in the workplace – specifically those of democracy and participation – are foundational to values in society more broadly; that is, we cannot have democracy in society without democracy in the workplace. Understanding how nonprofit organizations change to become less democratic and less community oriented is important if we care about the democratic soul of our nation.

Angela M. Eikenberry, PhD, D.B. and Paula Varner Professor, School of Public Administration, University of Nebraska at Omaha

Note

1 Thomas, D. (27th September, 2019). Brexit has turned into a war against the soul of the UK (accessed: 17.08.2020). https://www.independent.co.uk/voices/letters/boris-johnson-brexit-supreme-court-general-election-pensions-a9102831.html

Preface

My interest in this study developed alongside unprecedented change in the organization ("the association") in which I had worked for about a decade. My long-established sense of "how it feels to work around here" was being eroded – fast – and I felt unbalanced, rudderless, with only my internal compass to navigate my work activity: a compass that seemed increasingly at odds with any external point of reference. Initially I put it down to being a newly promoted Director, and the fact that I was now exposed to entirely different types of conversations from a different vantage point than the one I "knew." Or perhaps I had been thrown off balance by the appointment of a new Chief Executive, with a fundamentally different vision for the association, just shortly after my promotion and I simply needed to get used to their ways of working.

I attended a conference about 18 months after the new CEO started, where I listened to the keynote speaker talk about how, what they referred to as the "interplay of intentions," can shape the politics, activities, outcomes and experience of everyday life in organizations. At that moment, I realized that my sense of change was more deep-rooted than me having a new role, or having to get used to someone else's working style. It was about someone with a very clear set of intentions that seemed to contravene the association's established norms, the values I had held and been socialized with throughout my career (public service) and the power of office to make change happen. As time passed, I became increasingly fascinated by how one individual could have such an impact, so quickly, within an organization that had been around for over a century, which they did not (and could not) "own," and which was legally bound to its (social) purpose by virtue of Royal Charter and Charity status. I was also intrigued by how efforts to transform the association "landed" with others who inhabited it, how they contributed to organizational change and/or circumvented it by defending and repairing existing beliefs and practices. At the same time, I commenced a Doctorate in Business Administration (DBA), met Tracey, my co-author, and decided to use my curiosity as the platform for a formal programme of doctoral research. We wish to state at the outset that this is not a book about CEOs; it is a book about organizational change and how it is brought about. The CEO specifically, and senior managers more generally (including my own role as such), nevertheless receive a good deal of scrutiny, simply because of their centrality to change efforts in work organizations. To protect and honor those involved, the characters have been given fictitious names.

Many people have asked me why I chose to do a high-level, lengthy programme of study at the same time as holding a demanding, senior job role. In truth, a few things led me down this route. I was in my early 40s, and with my children growing up, I felt "stuck in a rut" and wanted a change. I had always enjoyed the process of learning, of being exposed to new theories and concepts and thinking about their application in a real-life context, but had previously discounted the idea of doing a PhD – largely because I felt I had nothing unique to contribute. It was a happenstance of three events that brought me to the DBA. First, I was speaking to my work-mentor about PhDs and they challenged my thinking by asking if it would make a difference if I framed a PhD as being less about saying something new and more about having a question I wanted to find answers to. I certainly did have questions that were consuming me, so I began to explore how PhDs work and turned to the university where I completed my Masters programme. Meeting up with a former tutor for a coffee, I outlined what I was experiencing personally and at work and they introduced me to the concept of a DBA, explaining how I could use this both as a personal development journey and to help answer my practice-related puzzle.

Remaining true to the spirit in which I undertook this journey, we are deliberate in using theory to situate and extend but not dominate our analysis of organizational change. In particular, we set the theoretical scene within the introductory chapter and return to it in concluding the book. The intervening chapters allow the transformation of the association, and its implications for various aspects of organizing (governance, strategy, structure, leadership etc.), to take centre stage. We should nevertheless acknowledge that such aspects of organizing are themselves the theoretical constructs of organization and management scholars; we see theory and practice as mutually constitutive. Stylistically, we engage academic literature in the intervening chapters where we feel it enhances our treatment of the issue at hand by enabling us to revisit situated events in a more analytical manner and/or to signpost you, the reader, to further material.

As for my own research journey, it was at times cathartic insofar as it became my personal process of sensemaking about my professional life. It was rich in learning and change; my worldview evolved and my long-held commitment to the existence of an absolute to guide management decisions and action was on shaky ground. "World-making" fast became an agentic, negotiated and contested process and understanding it a far more complex task. Tracey would act as the first critical audience for my own sensemaking. We would spend hours talking through particular, seemingly significant, incidents or just the minutia of daily life at the association. Early in my doctoral studies, she introduced me to institutional theory and, in particular, the strands of literature relating to institutional logics (sets of material practices and symbolic constructions that form particular organizing principles), hybrid organizations (those comprised more than one logic – e.g. community, corporate) and institutional work (purposive action to create, maintain or disrupt institutions and/or organizing logics).

Being able to "theorize" as well as "live" life in the association helped me to achieve some critical distance in my role as researcher, providing the framework for me to see the association as the *object* of my study and organizational change through the lens of institutionalism as the *subject*. I began to view the organization as having competing sets of logics, which resulted in an almost perpetual state of war, with the champions of each logic seeking to overturn the other (often, but not always, the "old guard" versus the "new guard"). Through the lens of institutional work, I came to understand the actions that individuals took to maintain, reject and transform institutional logics and how we, as individuals, can be both powerful agents of change and unassuming cultural dopes. It was at times fascinating, and at times demoralizing as I became sensitized to the "interplay of intentions," and outright "argy-bargy," involved in processes of change.

There was, however, a cost to my new vantage point. As my sensemaking of what was going on evolved, I began to understand power, persuasion and authority in profoundly different ways and began to experience significant internal tensions. Greater commercialism and associated behaviours that went with it were in constant conflict with my framing of the association's purpose and the personal values I tried to live by as a colleague and a manager. I often found myself trying to mitigate the implications of our new way of being for myself, for others and for the association's culture. A close friend and long-term colleague once referred to me as a "double-agent," a description that rang true with my own experience; another asked how I was able to sleep at night. Although the question came from a fellow Director, and in the context of him reflecting on his own ability to do just that, it deepened my unease at my potential complicity in supporting and perpetuating what I considered illegitimate managerial action in a non-profit context and "on my watch." This concern and my unwillingness to accept the new order ultimately led to me leaving the association as it became too costly on a personal level and un-resolvable on a practical one.

I state this upfront, not as an act of indulgence, but as context that represents an integral part of and pivotal moment in my professional life. Rather than attempting, artificially, to write my personal experience out of the research account we present in this book, I have made a deliberate effort to reveal, interweave and critically reflect upon my "professional hand" in our telling of the association's story. As a means to bring "involvement-detachment" into a productive balance, Tracey took the lead on re-analyzing, re-drafting and restructuring material from my doctoral study for the specific purposes of this book. We do not strive for or claim absolute objectivity (in our view a fallacy that lies behind the notion of "scientific research" about the social world), but instead try to provide a rigorous account that gets closer to the "realities" of managerial work. We hope you enjoy our tale of the field.

Acknowledgements

The research underpinning this book was undertaken for a part-time doctoral programme of study. It would not have been possible without the generous support of the focal organization – my sincere thanks are given to the then CEO and Trustee Board for approving the fieldwork and to my colleagues for their enthusiastic, candid participation. I also give thanks to my supervisory team: Dr Katherine Gardiner of Sheffield Hallam University as my Director of Studies and my second supervisor Professor Penny Dick, University of Sheffield.

Carole Bain

There are so many people who contributed to making this project happen. I am particularly indebted to Carole for years of diligently collecting and collating field data, to Susanne Tietze for convincing me I "had a book in me" after all, to Angela Eikenberry, Susanne Tietze and Chris Gallagher for commenting on early drafts, and to Brianna Ascher of Routledge for seeing potential in our project.

Tracey M. Coule

List of Abbreviations

AVE	Advertising Value Equivalent
COS	Charities Organisation Society
CEO	Chief Executive Officer
CCPMO	Consultative Committee for Professional Management Organisations
DGVO	Director General of Voluntary Organisations
EGM	Extra-ordinary General Meeting
FD	Financial Director
FY(s)	Financial Year(s)
HR	Human Resources
ICT	Information Communication Technology
IP	Intellectual Property
LTIP	Long-term Incentive Plan
MD	Managing Director
ME	Medium Enterprise
NCVO	National Council for Voluntary Organisations
NFR	Net Financial Return
NPM	New Public Management
PA	Personal Assistant
PR	Public Relations
SLT	Senior Leadership Team
SME	Small-to-Medium Enterprise
UK	United Kingdom
WFOE	Wholly Foreign-Owned Enterprise

1 Introduction

Nonprofit organizations are conventionally positioned as generators of social and cultural forms of capital for the common good. As such they occupy a different space from other types of organization, such as the corporate firm, which exist primarily to generate economic capital for private owners/shareholders (see Bourdieu (1986) for a full exploration of economic, social and cultural forms of capital). Recent years, however, have seen professionalization promoted widely by funders, policy-makers and nonprofit practitioners across the globe. At the same time, there has been an increasing cross-over of employees from private and public bodies into nonprofits. But do such shifts open up space for the wholesale importation of managerialism into the nonprofit sphere? Are nonprofits at risk of being reconstituted as primarily economic entities, serving the interests of a leadership elite? How are such changes in an organization's trajectory brought about? What are the consequences for trustees, staff, members and the nature of managerial work?

Our aim in this book is to engage with critical questions such as these through a unique insider account of one professional association (referred to from here on as "the association" or "the institute") experiencing unprecedented changes that challenge its very reason for being. Drawing on a 3-year field study, we narrate organizational inhabitants' struggles in their search for purpose and analyse the myriad changes within different aspects of organizing. These include structure, strategizing, pay and reward, governance and leadership. Our motivation is to chronicle, with unswerving fidelity to inhabitants' experiences, the often unspoken, unrevealed aspects of organizing and managing work in nonprofits. The shadow side of organization is usually only ever witnessed *and* documented by those simultaneously living *and* researching life in organizations over extended time periods. Yet, such accounts are powerful, and perhaps unique, in returning us to the potential for (in) humanity in organization. We hope our story of the association prompts engagement with the bigger questions (and a profoundly human view) of nonprofit organization among those who manage, govern and study nonprofits. We should not concern ourselves with *what* "good" is being done *by* nonprofits at the expense of considering the ethics of *how* things get done *in* nonprofits.

Professionalization, Competing Institutional Logics and the Emergence of Organizational Hybridity

Before telling our story of the association's transformation, we wish to set the wider scene. To do this, we draw on key theoretical ideas from institutionalism and scholarship regarding the historical and contemporary societal role of nonprofits vis-à-vis the state and the market. This is important for understanding nonprofit professionalization and the emergence of hybrid forms of organizing (those *comprising more than one cultural logic)* because such scholarship goes some way in explaining the macro-level conditions within which these developments have occurred.

Voluntary action or nonprofit organizing has played a major role in many Western democracies for centuries. In the U.K. specifically, it developed from a source of locally organized social action and welfare provision that was not the stuff of "high politics" in Victorian Britain (Lewis, 1996) to an extension of state apparatus through the hyperactive mainstreaming of the 'third sector' into public policy under New Labour (1997–2010) (Kendall, 2010). In its earliest guises, voluntary action addressed poverty and tackled the underlying causes of inequality and disadvantage (Tilly, 2005; Rochester, 2014). It did so through what Beveridge (1948) later referred to as a top-down philanthropic impulse (e.g. charitable trusts financed by private wealth) and a bottom-up mutual aid impulse (e.g. friendly societies, social movements and the like). We suggest such social action was underpinned by a "community logic" (Marquis et al., 2011). A community logic or "institutional order" is founded upon a commitment to community values and ideology, personal investment in the collective good, cooperation, trust and reciprocity, though not devoid of ego satisfaction and reputation factors (Thornton et al., 2012; also see Mohan & Breeze, 2015 on The Logic of Charity).

The first wave of professionalization emerged in the latter half of the 19th century and early 20th century. Attempts to better co-ordinate nonprofit organizing through development of the precursors to what we now refer to as "infrastructure" or intermediary bodies date as far back as 1869, with the founding of the Charities Organisation Society (COS). This intensified further in the early 20th century with developments in the state's responsibilities for welfare services, representing a shift in the institutional logic of the state. The liberal welfare reforms of the 1906–1911 Lloyd George administration involved state intervention in what was previously the territory of voluntarism. This in turn created an imperative for nonprofits to acquire a national presence to influence new governmental actors on the welfare stage and follow the state in adopting a bureaucratic model of organization (Penn, 2011). Grant (2011; 2014) traces further impetus to the professionalization of nonprofit organizing to its contribution to wartime social stability during World War I (1911–1914). In particular, he notes the turn from "amateur" to professional, paid social workers; the invention and expansion of modern fundraising methods; the emergence of state attempts to better co-ordinate voluntarism and, relatedly, the development of institutions that exist to promote mutually supportive links between statutory and voluntary "sectors." These included the War Office's appointment of a Director General of Voluntary Organizations (DGVO) in 1915 and establishment of a Council of Social Service in 1919, which superseded the COS and later became the National Council for Voluntary Organisations (NCVO) (See Coule & Bennett (2018) for a historical account of state–voluntary relations).

A second wave of professionalization ensued following changes in social attitudes in the 1970s, when citizens increasingly became unwilling to pay towards the welfare of others. This provided impetus for the 1979 U.K. Conservative government to undertake large-scale reforms to Labour's post-World War II "welfare state" architecture, which was based on the influential Beveridge report of 1942. These reforms involved development of an "enterprise culture" involving tax cuts, privatization of government services, deregulation and public spending cuts. The associated introduction of New Public Management (NPM) in the late 1980s resulted in a system of public services organized on a "market logic," emphasizing competition, consumer choice and efficiency (Coule & Patmore, 2013). Following the global economic crisis, the U.K. Conservative–Liberal Democrats Coalition (2010–2015) quickly began to dismantle New Labour's "partnership" apparatus and positioned the state's role as a (welfare) market creator and reformer. Significantly, it brought the state's treatment of nonprofits in line with that of private corporations, cuing the expectation that they should embody the "ideal type" of public service delivery agent – that of a professional and enterprising entity (Coule & Bennett, 2016). The state not only displayed a disinterest in nonprofit advocacy/campaigning for the most vulnerable in society, but also suffered heated media attacks for gagging nonprofits through specific clauses in contracts between government and nonprofit providers, alongside the broader ranging Lobbying Act. In a review of the Civil Society Strategy of 2018, Bennett et al. (2019) point to the Tory government's latest discursive affront including the use of the adjective "traditional" to describe those parts of the "social sector" that include "individual philanthropists, trusts and foundations" (HM Government, 2018, p.19), thus inciting us to see this as nostalgic, archaic and serving a bygone era. This is held in contrast to the alternative, cotemporary ways in which social value is produced through "social enterprises, mutuals and mission-led businesses" (p.18) and situates mission-led businesses as the driving force of social transformation and civil society Bennett 2019.

The culture of valuing corporate and entrepreneurial approaches above alternatives is not unique to the U.K. (Eikenberry, 2009): "the framework of marketization today is increasingly dominated by the core principles of global neoliberalism and its pervasive faith in the market and business-based approaches and solutions" (Dart, 2004, p. 418). With the global decline of other economic models, "neoliberal economics has become the prevailing position for much of the world" (Simpson & Cheney, 2007, p. 192). Citizens in Western democracies now live in what has been referred to as the hollow state (Milward & Provan, 2000) or the shadow state (Wolch, 1990). In other words, we live in societies with increasingly privatized governments that contract the provision of public goods to nonprofits and private corporations in place of state services (Salamon, 1995).

This globalized market-based approach to public management is well documented (Salamon, 1993; Eikenberry & Kluver, 2004; Eikenberry, 2009; Macmillan & Livingstone, 2015; Macmillan, 2017), with concerns expressed for its negative impact on democratic accountability and ideals (e.g. fairness, justice), citizenship and action for the collective public interest (Box, 1999; Box et al. 2001; deLeon & Denhardt, 2000; Denhardt & Denhardt, 2000; King & Stivers, 1998; Terry, 1998). The entrepreneurialism and satisfaction of individual client needs at the heart of the approach, alongside the adoption of private market values and practices among nonprofits themselves (Weisbrod, 1998), has led to the marketization of the nonprofit arena (Salamon, 1997). Ensuing "'major marketization trends" such as commercial revenue generation, contract competition, the influence of new and emerging donors, social entrepreneurship, the market's co-optation of the philanthropic impulse through consumption (e.g. cause-related marketing) and celebrity philanthropy are equally well examined (Eikenberry and Kluver, 2004 p. 132; King, 2006; Nickel & Eikenberry, 2009).

In the contemporary era then, nonprofit organizations are faced with significant institutional complexity (Greenwood et al., 2011). At a macro or societal level, there are state, market and community logics (Thornton et al., 2012; Jay, 2013; Pache & Santos, 2013; Meyer et al., 2014; Skelcher & Smith, 2015), underpinned by divergent "sets of material practices and symbolic constructions" that constitute their "organizing principles" (Friedland & Alford, 1991, pp. 248–249). Such complexity has the potential to result in what institutional scholars commonly refer to as "hybrid organizations" that are "subject to multiple regulatory regimes, embedded within multiple normative orders, and/or constituted by more than one cultural logic" (Kraatz & Block, 2008, p. 2).

Some organization theorists are pessimistic about the long-term survival prospects of hybrids, due to them being inherent arenas of contradiction (Scott & Meyer, 1991; Scott, 2001; Battilana & Dorado, 2010; Turco, 2012) that become "blocked, dysfunctional, and unable to resolve tensions between competing logics" (Skelcher & Smith, 2014, p. 440). Because a hybrid organization must concurrently negotiate the rules of the game in multiple, contradictory games (Heimer, 1999; Zilber, 2002; Glynn, 2008) it is "so many different things to so many different people that it must, of necessity, be partially at war with itself" (Kerr, 1963, p. 8). Others, who study nonprofit organizational forms specifically, suggest hybridity is an inevitable and permanent characteristic of nonprofits (Brandsen et al., 2005; Billis, 2010) and that they possess the ability to blend and synergize different logics (Haveman & Rao, 2006; Galaskiewicz & Barringer, 2012; Jay, 2013; Jäger & Schröer, 2014; Skelcher & Smith, 2014).

As we will show in the coming chapters, it is our experience that there are perpetual (moral) struggles over what might constitute "good" or "bad," "right" or "wrong" or appropriate ways of thinking and acting within systems of meaning that are based on conflicting assumptions about the nature of the world, human beings and work organizations. It is also our sense that the macro-level accounts of institutional change we have narrated so far provide useful insights into the contexts that encourage particular organizational forms, structures, cultures and practices to flourish. It helps us understand the role of institutional logics in the trend for nonprofits to become business-like, at least in the Global North (See Maier et al., 2016 for a comprehensive review of this phenomenon). To summarize, we have suggested in this section that the professionalization of the nonprofit world has occurred at the intersection of state, community and market logics, as the boundaries between and roles within these domains have become increasingly blurred and fluid over time. This has, at least in part, led to the rise of hybrid organizations (Minkoff, 2002; Evers, 2005; Smith, 2014; Mullins & Skelcher, 2018). What such macro explanations of change cannot provide is insight into how hybridity is managed at the organizational level or what individual managers "do" to shape organizational life and work towards particular social orders. This requires examination of the day-to-day managerial work within organizations, to which we now turn.

The Coming of Age of Managerial Work in Nonprofit Organizing

The proclaimed move from "amateur do-gooders" to "professional entities" has been accompanied by the appointment of paid managers in many formalized nonprofit organizations. Additionally, there has been an increase in the number of Schools of Business and Public Administration offering graduate degrees in Nonprofit Management, often targeted at the occupants of managerial roles. The management education within such schools, however, has been criticized for its narrow, technocratic focus on "management science." Critics have pointed to its role in the further entrenchment of the managerialization of the world (Alvesson & Deetz, 2000; Adler et al., 2008), the marginalization of alternative forms of organizing and the promotion of neo-liberal capitalism with all its social injustices and planetary consequences (Parker, 2018). As Ghoshal (2005, p. 76) puts it:

> "Academic research related to the conduct of business and management has had some very significant and negative influences on the practice of management ... by propagating ideologically inspired amoral theories, business schools have actively freed their students from any sense of moral responsibility."

One might expect specialist nonprofit courses to be somehow different; more cognizant about issues of public good, sustainability and a broader, more questioning approach perhaps. Yet recent work has shown that research on nonprofit organizing – the basis for many of these courses – has become increasingly conservative and mainstream in nature (Coule et al., 2020). Given the now common migration of managerial staff between "sectors," it is arguably even more important to equip management students to recognize and make reflective choices about the potentially oppressive, exploitative nature of managerial work (Adler et al., 2008) through a more critical pedagogy than is prevalent.

Such transitions from public administration and/or the corporate to the nonprofit world offer further opportunity for the professionalization and managerialization of nonprofits, as leaders "carry" the institutional logic with which they are socialized (Battilana & Dorado, 2010). Spending time within and managing organizations that are influenced by one institutional order or another, shapes individuals' sense of self and identity – conditioning understandings of who they are, particular modes of thinking, acting and talking and their perceived legitimacy (Weick, 1993; Lok, 2010; Gioia et al., 2013). In such contexts, it is all too easy for managerialist assumptions based on a narrow means–end rationality, in which nonprofit activity is solely judged on the efficient use of public (i.e. taxpayers') funds, to become an unquestioned social good above other ends (Alexander & Weiner, 1998). As King & Griffin (2019) usefully remind us, workplace democracy literature presents a serious challenge to the assumption that "managerialism and business-like practices are the most efficient and effective way of organizing" and the presentation of "efficiency and productivity as unquestionable virtues which should be the overriding aim of nonprofit activity" (p. 914). Rather, they argue, through ethics-based justification, that workplace democracy can be seen as holding intrinsic value in and of itself through producing exactly the type of society nonprofits often claim to want to produce within their mission (also see Land & King, 2014; Reedy et al., 2016).

The actions of individuals and groups within organizations, alongside the societal conditions narrated in the previous section, can provide fertile ground for the wholesale importation of corporate and/or bureaucratic ideologies and practices into the nonprofit realm. By way of example, King (2017) explored how socialization with other nonprofit managers and the practices associated with *being* a manager (e.g. evaluation, monitoring and reporting) governed him towards identifying as a "professional" and away from his activist ideological origins. From an activist perspective, evaluation and constructions of "organizational effectiveness" would be considered political acts rather than objective activities. Similarly, Metzendorf & Cnaan (1992) demonstrate how volunteer labour in feminist organizations can be a form of exploitation that undermines the very ideology the organization exists to advance. There are indeed numerous articles that challenge the notion that nonprofit organization actually produces the social benefits for which it is celebrated. Instead, they show that it can reflect and perpetuate social stratifications (Rosenzweig, 1977), promote cultural imperialism (Lenkersdorf, 1976), colonialism (Lagerspetz et al., 2002), fascism (Berman, 1997), be oligarchic and serve as a mechanism for elites to justify (class) inequalities and social relations (Bolduc, 1980; Lansley, 1996). This serves to remind us that "the social benefits that nonprofits can produce are accomplishments, not foundational features" (Coule et al., 2020, p.13). We show in this book that such social benefits may become more difficult to realize in the face of increasing hybridity and in contexts where "professionalism" is taken as synonymous with "commercialism."

One of the key challenges of managerial work within a hybrid organization is navigating the legitimacy dilemma – what constitutes "desirable, proper, or appropriate [actions]" for a hybrid entity, when they exist within multiple and contradictory "socially constructed system[s] of norms, values, beliefs, and definitions" (Suchman, 1995, p. 574)? The risks associated with doing this "badly" for nonprofits include: mission drift; poor accountability to stakeholders; having a marginalized majority; having significant structural, political, symbolic and ethical issues, and growing schisms between proponents of different logics (Battilana & Dorado, 2010; Ellis Paine et al., 2010; Turco, 2012; Chell et al., 2016; Ebrahim et al., 2014; Mongelli et al., 2019; Ometto et al., 2019).

So, what strategic responses have managers devised in attempting to balance or accommodate competing logics within organizations? One strategy is "decoupling" or "compartmentalising," where organizations ceremonially or symbolically conform to the prescriptions defined by the institutional environment through organizational policies, but do not attempt seriously to implement them in practice (Meyer & Rowan, 1977; Scott, 1983; Westphal & Zajac, 1999; Boxenbaum & Jonsson, 2008; Tilcsik, 2010; Bromley & Powell, 2012). Such compartmentalization is challenging and perhaps over simplistic, given that attempts to conform with the demands of one institutional order are inevitably visible to constituencies who identify with another (Stryker & Burke, 2000; Glynn, 2000; Pache & Santos, 2013). A second approach is "selective coupling" or "logic combination." This is common when significant complementarities exist between institutionally prescribed identities; in other words, when the organization's ability to successfully be one thing enhances its ability to be another (Kraatz & Block, 2008; Pache & Santos, 2010; 2013). The third strategic response that has seen much attention from organization theorists is "compromising," and is said to occur most often when organizations need to placate diverse external constituent groups (Kraatz & Block, 2008; Oliver, 1991; Pache & Santos, 2013). Compromising involves crafting an acceptable balance between competing logics by conforming to minimum standards of what is expected within each logic and/or bargaining with stakeholders so that they alter their demands (Scott, 1983). One of the major risks is that the organization may not fully secure support from important referents or stakeholders, particularly over the long term (Pache & Santos, 2013). Powell & Colyvas (2008) provide an informative example involving a nonprofit that created a separate trading company; referents (politicians, media and competitors) subsequently became highly critical of both entities, challenging their legitimacy, legality and lack of transparency.

This type of organizational analysis usefully highlights the socio-structural challenges of hybridity and the strategies that managers in nonprofit hybrids may adopt in order to cope with it. The danger, however, is that institutional logics become reified as deterministic social structures that drive organizations in an apparently inevitable direction and strategic organizational responses become disembodied from agentic actors. In other words, the thoughts and actions of human agents in making sense of and acting within the pluralistic world they are faced with is largely absent from accounts of strategic responses to institutional complexity. Given our interests, we turn to the concept of "institutional work," defined as purposive action aimed at creating, maintaining or disrupting institutions (Lawrence & Suddaby, 2006). This area represents the "new buds of research" on the topic of institutional logics (Lounsbury & Boxenbaum, 2013, p. 3) but is core to understanding how people engage logics in the seemingly benign everyday talk and activities of managerial work, and how such engagement reproduces or transforms the rules of the game or the game itself (Lok, 2010; McPherson & Sauder, 2013; Smets et al., 2015).

What we are particularly interested in, in the context of this book, is the institutional work of managers that is directed towards the transformation (and defence) of organizing principles, and how those that inhabit the organization react to these change efforts. More specifically, we will elaborate the dynamic interplay of two types of institutional work involved in efforts to bring about and resist organizational change: identification work (performed to influence perceptions of and identification with organizational identity and purpose) and practice work (aimed at (re)defining, (re)developing, legitimating and diffusing practices associated with those logics). See Gawer & Phillips (2013) for a useful overview of these types of internally focused institutional work. Before we begin, some information on our positionality in relation to the study.

An Expressionist Tale of the Field: The Ethnographers' Hand

Although the writing of this book is a joint endeavor, the field study that underpins it was undertaken entirely by the second author. Thus, we use the terms *we* and *our* to represent our collective voice as co-authors and *I* and *my* to denote Carole as the embedded and embodied ethnographer (and manager). I went into the field as a "researching manager" to understand better the processes of "world making" (Schwandt, 1994) within a hybrid organization. In other words, how inhabitants of the association (including myself) established and re-established the meanings used to organize experiences in a complex work environment. I was not looking for a universal *truth* about the world of nonprofit organization and management. I wanted, as Watson (2001, p. 5) puts it, to provide an account "in a way which might be closer to the 'realities' of the managerial experience than much of what is on offer in management textbooks and courses." This required "an anthropological frame of mind" (Ericsson & Kostera, 2020, p. 2) involving openness to new realities and meanings, persistent curiosity and problematization of all social worlds (Czarniawska-Joerges, 1992).

The tale you are about to read emerges from an overt but embedded ethnography. I spent 3 years in the field paying close and intensive attention to organizational life using a number of methods: interviews (or purposeful conversations), document analysis and extensive participant observation. But I had been a "complete member" (Brannick *&* Coghlan, 2007) of the organization as an employee and thus in the "waiting room" (Mannay & Morgan, 2015) for some 14 years prior to starting data collection. As such, I was able to take advantage of prolonged personal presence and the attention, immersion and experience of the field that comes with it (Pachirat, 2018). Despite the extensive, detailed preparations necessary to secure ethics approval for the study prior to entering the field (e.g. obtaining organizational approval, detailing measures to ensure overt research, voluntary participation, informed consent and secure data management), the margins between being an organizational inhabitant and being an ethnographer were at times fuzzy and not easily delineated. As Hynes (2012, pp. 84–85) usefully puts it, there is a "shifting sense of self as both the subject and the object of research … belonging to the research and being outside it."

The pursuit of critical distance and rigor in my analysis and interpretation as a researcher expanded the boundaries of my thinking and actions as a senior manager, and played no small part in my eventual departure from the organization. As an embedded ethnographer, I recognized early on that I needed to deliberately and systematically take steps to challenge my routines within and perspectives on the organization and its activities as a long-term inhabitant. I was, after all, a native going researcher rather than a researcher gone native, making my ability to turn back upon and take account of myself an important part of the research process (Weick, 2002).

To this end, as I entered the field in my new role (as researcher), I invited a colleague from the graduate programme, who I knew to be very reflective and thoughtful, to walk around the building with me and just "say what you see." What was striking, was his attention to the "symbolic" – the solid wood plaques carved with previous presidents' names that were reminiscent of golf clubs and tradition, juxtaposed elsewhere with colorful maps of the world evoking the image of a modern, global company. These symbols had become so naturalized to me that I barely noticed them – until the walk around that is. I routinely wrote in a reflective journal about significant events relating to my research (what I thought about them, how they made me feel, how I handled them as a manager), the interaction between my dual roles and identities, and how this might be playing out in the analysis and interpretation of ethnographic data. These reflections, alongside interpretations of events and organizational life, were presented to Tracey and my research supervisors to stimulate the search for alternative interpretations and refinement of ideas. The many hours Tracey and I would spend talking through particular, seemingly significant incidents, or just the minutia of daily life at the association, provided a degree of abstraction from my professional context and counterbalanced my embeddedness.

As a product of ethnography, this book is not a natural or unproblematic act, and it is important to reveal our hand in the research account. Van Maanen (1989) aptly shows that we cannot represent the "Other" in any terms but our own. Ethnographic data do not "speak for itself" and experience is evidence (Yanow & Geuijen, 2009). In representing social reality within the association, we have chosen to focus concurrently on the fieldworker/manager (Carole) *and* the culture (or particular aspects of it) in writing this book. This produces, in Van Maanen's terms, an impressionist tale of the field, which explicitly attempts to bring the knower (privileged in confessional tales) and the known (privileged in realist tales) together in a representational form (see Van Maanen, 1989, for an extended and engaging account of different ethnographic approaches). The value of impressionist tales is assessed by criteria of narrative rationality such as interest, coherence and fidelity (Weick, 1989). In attempting to meet these criteria, we represent organizational life from the perspective of the people who lived it (in anonymized form), in their own words, throughout subsequent chapters. This includes autoethnographic elements that attempt to embody my own managerial experiences in the analytical narrative rather than attempting, artificially, to write my "professional hand" out of the account.

In attempting to bring "involvement-detachment" into a productive balance in producing this text, Tracey took the lead on re-analyzing, re-drafting and re-structuring material from my doctoral study for the specific purposes of this book. The chapters then underwent introspective interrogation by me, from the vantage point of both senior manager and embedded ethnographer, and by a former colleague at the association. A similar process had already taken place during the original period of doctoral study but involving an internal reviewer group (see Appendix 1). This was core to assessing and ensuring the fidelity of our account and interpretations to "how it feels around here." It was also a means of intentionally "shifting attention from [our] own concerns and agendas outwards, to the Other" (Ericsson & Kostera, 2020, p. 6).

Regardless of our quest for rigorous scholarship, we do not lay claim to a neutral analysis. To do so would be misleading. We are sceptical of the moral defensibility and social sustainability of prevalent conceptions of and approaches to organization and management (Adler et al., 2008) generally, and the wholesale importation of corporate ideologies and practices into the nonprofit sphere specifically. It is important to note, however, that this book narrates one organization's trajectory within a specific, and now historical, period of time. Since the completion of the fieldwork, we understand there have been many changes to key role-holders at board, CEO and senior management levels and reversal of some of the decisions, processes and practices discussed here. In other words, the organization has likely been re-imagined and re-invented by now. Nevertheless, it offers the basis for a unique, insider account of the organizational processes and managerial work involved in organizational change as it unfolds *in situ*, over time. We also hope it holds the potential for a genuine re-thinking of power, persuasion and authority in nonprofit work. Taking inspiration from Ericsson & Kostera (2020) our approach to ethnography is both "a way of doing research and a way of writing for change" (p. 3).

On starting data collection, I initially focused on the general organizational context, paying attention to how people constituted the organization and its purpose, if they experienced and how they made sense of different sets of material practices and symbolic constructions (i.e. logics). This was an important step in establishing whether others experienced the interplay of divergent organizing principles and their consequences in similar ways to what I did. After that, I started to "follow the noise," particularly when it surfaced at managerial levels, which I was privilege to because of my own role in the hierarchy. My experience is that things get attention from senior managers when existing orders, practices and territories are perceived to be in question or under threat. In this sense, the research process itself rested on a "logic of discovery and happenstance rather than a logic of verification and planning" (Van Maanen, 2011 p. 219). The overall aim was to move beyond my own personal experience of incidents and subject myself to "a set of contingencies that play on others such that over time ... one can see, hear, feel and come to understand the kinds of response others display (and withhold) in particular social situations" (Van Maanen, 1989 p. 220). This was key to understanding the interplay between hybridity and change efforts, what managerial work is undertaken to transform and defend organizing logics, who influences this work and how, and what happens if individuals or groups of "insiders" do not see proffered logics as legitimate.

Data analysis was quite informal while in the field, followed by more formal, systematic analysis once data collection ceased. During the fieldwork phase, I developed free-flowing narratives to explore the often-divergent ways people constituted the organization and its purpose and how apparent conflict between divergent organizing logics played out among individuals, teams, functions and structures and within organizational processes (governance, strategy, decision-making, etc). To aid sensemaking I drew free-hand sketches, developing visual mind maps of who was involved, what roles they played, what was occurring and how different aspects of the incidents related to others and to organizational life more broadly. On completion of data collection, I (and then we) began systematically working through the data sources to develop the descriptions and theoretical accounts that feature in this book (see Appendix 1 for a more detailed account of data collection and analysis methods).

The structure of the book flows logically from our interest in hybridity, the nature of managerial work and the politics of change. Part I of the book looks at the hybrid world of the organization whereas part II examines the managerial work involved in transforming the organization's trajectory. Chapter 2 explores actors' struggles to make sense of organizational purpose in the face of divergent organizing logics. Chapter 3 highlights the contested, political nature of managerial work within this hybrid context. Chapter 4 explains the role of symbolism, rhetoric and strategizing in shaping the organization's trajectory away from its original (social) purpose. Having outlined the warzone-like culture that can be created by the search for purpose among contradictory organizing logics, we turn in Part II to the managerial work involved in transforming the organization's raison d'être and the myriad associated changes in organizational structure, processes and relations. Chapter 5 examines the changes to organizational, governance and managerial structures in pursuit of commercialization and growth. Chapter 6 considers changes to the pay and reward scheme in order to encourage loyalty to the (new) cause. Chapter 7 examines the measures taken to immobilize resistance from dissenters who threaten the perceived legitimacy of the new order. Chapter 8 examines the cultivation of a culture that enabled the CEO to lead away from purpose and get away with it. In the Conclusion, we return to our opening questions, summarizing what our story of the association tells us about managerialism in nonprofit organizations, about their potential to become reconstituted as economic entities, about how such transformations to organizational trajectories are brought about, and with what consequences for organizing and managing nonprofit work.

References

Adler, P. S., Forbes, L. C., & Willmott, H. (2008). Critical management studies. *The Academy of Management Annals*, *1*, 119–179.

Alexander, J. A., & Weiner, B. J. (1998). The adoption of the corporate governance model by nonprofit organizations. *Nonprofit Management & Leadership*, *8*, 223–242.

Alvesson, M., & Deetz, S. (2000). *Doing Critical Management Research*. London: Sage.

Battilana, J., & Dorado, S. (2010). Building sustainable hybrid organisations: The case of commercial microfinance organisations. *Academy of Management Journal*, *53*(6), 1419–1440.

Bennett, E., Coule, T., Damm, C., Dayson, C., Dean, J., & Macmillan, R. (2019). Civil society strategy: A policy review. *Voluntary Sector Review*, *10*(2), 213–223.

Berman, S. (1997). Civil society and the collapse of the Weimar Republic. *World Politics*, *49*(3), 401–429.

Beveridge, W. H. B. (1948). *Voluntary Action: A Report on Methods of Social Advance*. London: Allen & Unwin.

Beveridge, W. H. B. (1942). *Social Insurance and Allied Services. Report by Sir William Beveridge*. London, H.M. Stationery Office.

Billis, D. (2010). *Hybridge Organisations and the Third Sector*. New York, NY, USA: Palgrave MacMillan.

Bolduc, V. L. (1980). Representation and legitimacy in neighbourhood organizations: A case study. *Journal of Voluntary Action Research*, *9*(1–4), 165–178.

Bourdieu, P. (1986). The forms of capital. In J. G. Richardson, *Handbook of Theory and Research for the Sociology of Education* (pp. 241–258). Westport, NY, USA: Greenwood Press.

Box, R. C. (1999). Running government like a business: implications for public administration theory and practice. *American Review of Public Administration* *29*(1): 19–43.

Box Richard, C., Marshall, Gary S., Reed, B. J., & Reed, Christine M. (2001). New public management and substantive democracy. *Public Administration Review* *61*(5): 608–619.

Boxenbaum, E. & Jonsson, S. (2008). Isomorphism, diffusion and decoupling. In R. Grenwood, C. Oliver, K. Sahlin-Andersson, & R. Suddaby, *The Sage Handbook of Organisational Institutionalism* (pp. 78–98). Thousand Oaks, CA: SAGE.

Brandsen, T., van de Donk, W., & Putters, K. (2005). Griffins or chameleons? Hybridity as a permanent and inevitable characteristic of the third sector. *International Journal of Public Administration*, *28*(9–10), 749–765.

Brannick, T., & Coghlan, D. (2007). In defense of being native: The case for insider academic research. *Organizational Research Methods*, *1*, 59–74.

Bromley, P., & Powell, W. W. (2012). From smoke and mirrors to walking the talk: Decoupling in the contemporary world. *Academy of Management Annals*, *6*(1), 483–530.

Chell, E., Spence, L. J., Perrini, F., & Harris, J. D. (2016). Social enterprise and business ethics: Does social equal ethical? *Journal of Business Ethics*, *133*(4), 619–625.

Coule, T. M., & Bennett, E. (2018). State–voluntary relations in the contemporary welfare era: New politics or voluntary action as usual? *Nonprofit and Voluntary Sector Quarterly*. *47*(4_suppl.), 139S–158S.

Coule, T., & Bennett, E. (2016). Rhetoric, organizational category dynamics and institutional change: A study of the UK welfare state. *Public Administration*, *94*(4), 1059–1076.

Coule, T., & Patmore, B. (2013). Institutional logics, institutional work and service innovation in non-profit organizations. *Public Administration*, *94*(4), 980–997.

Coule, T. M., Dodge, J., & Eikenberry, A. M. (2020). Toward a typology of critical nonprofit studies: A literature review. *Nonprofit and Voluntary Sector Quarterly*, 1–29. doi: 10.1177/0899764020919807.

Czarniawska-Joerges, B. (1992). *Exploring Complex Organizations: A Cultural Perspective*. Newbury Park, CA: Sage.

Dart, R. (2004). The legitimacy of social enterprise. *Nonprofit Management & Leadership*, *14*, 411–424.

deLeon, L., & Denhardt, R. (2000). The political theory of reinvention. *Public Administration Review*, *60*(2), 89–97.

Denhardt, R. B., & Denhardt, J. V. (2000). The new public service: Serving rather than steering. *Public Administration Review*, *60*(6), 549–559.

Ebrahim, A., Battilana, J., & Mair, J. (2014). The governance of social enterprises: Mission drift and accountability challenges in hybrid organizations. *Research in Organizational Behavior*, *34*, 81–100.

Eikenberry, A. M. (2009). Refusing the market: A democratic discourse for voluntary and nonprofit organizations. *Nonprofit and Voluntary Sector Quarterly*, *38*(4), 582–596.

Eikenberry, A. M., & Kluver, J. D. (2004). Marketization of the nonprofit sector: Civil society at risk? *Public Administration Review*, *64*(2), 132–140.

Ellis Paine, A., Ockhenden, N., & Stuart, J. (2010). Volunteers in a hybrid organisation. In D. Billis, *Hybridge Organisations and the Third Sector* (p. 270). New York, NY, USA: Palgrave MacMillian.

Ericsson, D., & Kostera, M. (2020). Alterethnography: Reading and writing otherness in organizations. *Gender, Work and Organization*, *27*(6), 1–16. doi: 10.1111/gwao.12503.

Evers, A. (2005). Mixed welfare systems and hybrid organizations: Changes in the governance and provision of social services. *International Journal of Public Administration*, *28*(9–10), 737–748.

Friedland, R., & Alford, R. R. (1991). Bringing society back in: Symbols, practices and institutional contradictions. In W. Powell, & P. J. Dimaggio (Eds), *The New Institutionalism in Organizational Analysis* (pp. 232–263). Chicago, IL: University of Chicago Press.

Galaskiewicz, J., & Barringer, S. N. (2012). Social enterprise and social categories. In B. Gidron, & Y. Hasenfeld, *Social Enterprise: An Organizaional Perspective* (pp. 47–70). Basingstoke, England: Palgrave MacMillan.

Gawer, A., & Phillips, N. (2013). Institutional work as logic shift: The case of Intel's transformation to platform leader. *Organizational Studies*, *34*(8), 1035–1071.

Ghoshal, S. (2005). Bad management theories are destroying good management practices. *Academy of Management Learning and Education*, *4*(1), 75–91.

Gioia, D. A., Patvardhan, S. D., Hamilton, A. L., & Corley, K. G. (2013). Organizational identity formation and change. *The Academy of Management Annals*, *7*(1), 123–193.

Glynn, M. A. (2000). When cymbals become symbols: conflict over organizational identity within a symphony orchestra. *Organizational Science* , *11*(3), 285–298.

Glynn, M. A. (2008). Beyond constraint: How institutions enable identities. In R. Greenwood, C. Oliver, K. Sahlin-Andersson, & R. Suddaby, *The Sage Handbook of Organizational Institutionalism* (pp. 413–430). Thousand Oaks, CA: Sage.

Grant, P. (2011). Voluntarism and the impact of the First World War. In M. Hilton, & J. McKay (Eds), *The Ages of Voluntarism: How We Got to the Big Society*. Oxford: Oxford University Press.

Grant, P. (2014). *Philanthropy and Voluntary Action in the First World War: Mobilizing Charity*. New York: Routledge.

Greenwood, R., Raynard, M., Kodeih, F., Micellotta E. R., & Lounsbury, M. (2011). Institutional complexity and organizational responses. *The Academy of Management Annals*, *5*, 317–371.

Haveman, H. A., & Rao, H. (2006). Hybrid forms and the evolution of thrifts. *American Behavioural Scientist*, *49*(7), 974–986.

Heimer, C. A. (1999). Competing institutions: Law, medicine and family in neonatal intensive care. *Law & Society Review*, *33*(1): 17–66.

HM Government. (2018). *Civil Society Strategy: Building a Future that Works for Everyone*. London: Cabinet Office.

Hynes, K. (2012). Reflexivity in qualitative research. In G. Symon, & C. Cassell, *Qualitative Organizational Research: Core Methods and Current Challenges, Vol. 1* (pp. 72–89). London: Sage.

Jäger, U. P., & Schröer, A. (2014), Integrated organizational identity: A definition of hybrid organizations and a research agenda. *Voluntas*, *25*(5), 1281–1306.

Jay, J. (2013). Navigating paradox as a mechanism of change and innovation in hybrid organisations. *Academy of Management Journal*, *58*(1), 137–159.

Kendall. J. (2010). The U.K.: Ingredients in a hyperactive horizontal policy environment. In Kendall, J. (Ed.). *Handbook on Third Sector Policy in Europe: Multi-Level Processes and Organized Civil Society* (pp. 67–94). Cheltenham: Edward Elgar.

Kerr, C. (1963). *The Use of the University*. Cambridge, MA: Harvard University Press.

King, D. (2017). Becoming business-like: Governing the nonprofit professional. *Nonprofit and Voluntary Sector Quarterly*, *46*(2), 241–260.

King, D., & Griffin, M. (2019). Nonprofits as schools for democracy: The justifications for organizational democracy within nonprofit organizations. *Nonprofit & Voluntary Sector Quarterly*, *48*(5), 910–930.

King, S. (2006). *Pink Ribbons, Inc.: Breast Cancer and the Politics of Philanthropy*. Minneapolis: University of Minnesota Press.

King, C. S., & Stivers, C. (eds.) (1998). *Government Is Us: Public Administration in an Anti-Government Era*. Thousand Oaks, CA: Sage Publications.

Kraatz, M. S., & Block, E. S. (2008). Organizational implications of institutional pluralism. In R. Greenwood, C. Oliver, K. Sahlin-Andersson, & R. Suddaby (Eds.), *The SAGE Handbook of Organizational Institutionalism* (pp. 243–275). Thousand Oaks, CA: Sage Publications.

Lagerspetz, M., Rikmann, E., & Ruutsoo, R. (2002). The structure and resources of NGOs in Estonia. *Voluntas: International Journal of Voluntary and Nonprofit Organizations*, *13*(1), 73–87.

Land, C., & King, D. (2014). Organizing otherwise: Translating anarchism in a voluntary sector organization. *Ephemera*, *14*, 923–950.

Lansley, J. (1996). Membership participation and ideology in large voluntary organisations: The case of the National Trust. *Voluntas: International Journal of Voluntary and Nonprofit Organizations*, *7*(3), 221–240.

Lawrence, T. B., & Suddaby, R. (2006). Institutions and institutional work. In S. R. Clegg, T. B. Hardy, W. R. Lawrence, & W. R. Nord, *Handbook of Organizational Studies* (2nd ed.). London: Sage.

Lenkersdorf, C. (1976). Voluntary associations and social change in a Mexican context. *Journal of Voluntary Action Research*, *5*(3–4), 214–220.

Lewis, J. (1996). The boundary between voluntary and statutory social service in the late nineteenth and early twentieth centuries. *The Historical Journal*, *39*(1), 155–177.

Lok, J. (2010). Institutional logics as identity projects. *Academy of Management Journal*, *53*(6), 1305–1335.

Lounsbury, M., & Boxenbaum, E. (2013). Institutional logics in action, Part A. *Research in the Sociology of Organizations*, *39A*, 3–22.

Macmillan, R. (2017). Talking up the voluntary sector in criminal justice: Market making in rehabilitation. In Rees, J., & Mullins, D. (Eds), *The Third Sector Delivering Public Services: Developments, Innovations and Challenges* (pp.237–256). Bristol: Policy Press.

Macmillan, R., & Livingstone, I. (2015). More than a provider: The voluntary sector and market diversity in criminal justice. *Voluntary Sector Review*, *6*(2), 221–230.

Maier, F., Meyer, M., & Steinbereithner, M. (2016). Nonprofit organizations becoming business-like: A systematic review. *Nonprofit and Voluntary Sector Quarterly*, *45*(1), 64–86.

Mannay, D., & Morgan, M. (2015). Doing ethnography or applying qualitative techniques? Reflections from the waiting field. *Qualitative Research*, *15*(2), 166–182.

Marquis, C., Lounsbury, M., & Greenwood, R. (2011). Introduction: Community as an institutional order and a type of organizing. In Marquis, C., Lounsbury, M., & Greenwood, R. (Eds), *Communities and Organizations (Research in the Sociology of Organizations, Vol 33)* (pp. ix–xxvii). Emerald: Bingley.

McPherson, C. M., & Sauder, M. (2013). Logics in action: Managing institutional complexity in a drug court. *Administrative Science Quarterly*, *58*, 165–196.

Metzendorf, D., & Cnaan, R. A. (1992). Volunteers in feminist organizations. *Nonprofit Management and Leadership*, 2, 255–269.

Meyer, J. W., & Rowan, B. (1977). Institutionalized organizations: Formal structure as myth and ceremony. *American Journal of Sociology*, *83*(2), 340–363.

Meyer, R. E., Egger-Peitler, I., Hollerer, M. A., & Hammerschmid, G. (2014). Of bureaucrats and passionate public managers: Institutional logics, executive identities, and public service motivation. *Public Administration*, 92(4), 861–885.

Milward, H. B., & Provan, K. (2000). Governing the hollow state. *Journal of Public Administration Research and Theory*, 6, 193–195.

Minkoff, D. C. (2002). The emergence of hybrid organizational forms: Combining identity-based service provision and political action. *Nonprofit and Voluntary Sector Quarterly*, *31*(3), 377–401.

Mohan, J., & Breeze, B. (2015). *The Logic of Charity: Great Expectations in Hard Times*. Basingstoke: Palgrave Macmillan.

Mongelli, L., Rullani, F., Ramus, T., & Rimac, T. (2019). The bright side of hybridity: Exploring how social enterprises manage and leverage their hybrid nature. *Journal of Business Ethics*, *159*(2), 301–305.

Mullins, C., & Skelcher, C. (2018). The impact of societal-level institutional logics on hybridity: Evidence from nonprofit organizations in England and France. *Voluntas: International Journal of Voluntary and Nonprofit Organizations*, *29*, 911–924.

Nickel, P. M., & Eikenberry, A. M. (2009). A critique of the discourse of marketized philanthropy. *American Behavioral Scientist*, *52*, 974–989.

Oliver, C. (1991). Strategic responses to institutional processes. *Adminstrative Science Quarterly*, *16*, 145–176.

Ometto, M. P., Gegenhuber, T., & Winter, J. (2019). From balancing missions to mission drift: The role of the institutional context, spaces and compartmentalization in the scaling of social enterprise. *Business and Society*, *58*(5), 1003–1046.

Pache, A., & Santos, F. (2013). Inside the hybrid organization: Selective coupling as a response to competing institutional logics. *Academy of Management Journal*, *56*(4), 972–1001.

Pachirat, T. (2018). *Among Wolves: Ethnography and the Immersive Study of Power*. New York, NY: Routledge.

Parker, M. (2018). *Shut Down the Business School: What's Wrong with Management Education*. London: Pluto Press.

Penn, A. (2011). A social historical approach to understanding organisational issues in voluntary action. In C. Rochester, G. Gosling, A. Penn, & M. Zimmeck (Eds), *Understanding the Roots of Voluntary Action* (pp. 17–29). Eastbourne: Sussex Academic Press.

Powell, W. W., & Colyvas, J. A. (2008). Microfoundations of institutional theory. In R. Grenwood, C. Oliver, K. Sahlin, & R. Suddaby, *The Sage Handbook of Organizational Institutionalism* (pp. 276–288). Thousand Oaks, CA: SAGE - Business and Economics.

Reedy, P., King, D., & Coupland, C. (2016). Organizing for individuation: Alternative organizing, politics and new identities. *Organization Studies*, *37*, 1553–1573.

Rochester, C. (2014). Revisiting the Roots of Voluntary Action. Voluntary Action History Society Seminar, 13 January. Institute for Historical Research, London.

Rosenzweig, R. (1977). Boston Masons, 1900–1935: The lower middle class in a divided society. *Journal of Voluntary Action Research*, 6(3–4), 199–126.

Salamon, L. M. (1993). The marketization of welfare: Changing nonprofit and for-profit roles in the American welfare state. *Social Service Review* 67(1): 16–39.

Salamon, L. M. (1995). *Partners in Public Service: Government–Nonprofit Relations in the Modern Welfare State*. Baltimore: Johns Hopkins University Press.

Salamon, L. (1997). *Holding the Center: America's Nonprofit Sector at a Crossroads*. New York: Nathan Cummings Foundation.

Schwandt, T. A. (1994). Constructivists, interpretivist approaches to human enquiry. In *Handbook of Qualitative Research* (pp. 118–137). London: Sage.

Scott, W. R. (1983). Healthcare organizations in the 80s: The convergence of public and professional control systems. In J. Meyer, & W. R. Scott, *Organizational Environments: Ritual and Rationality* (pp. 99–114). Beverly Hills, CA: Sage.

Scott, W. R. (2001).*Institutions and Organizations* (2 ed.). Thousand Oaks: Sage.

Scott, W. R., & Meyer, J. W. (1991). The organization of societal sectors: Propositions and early evidence. In W. W. Powell, & P. J. DiMaggio (Eds), *The New Institutionalism in Organizational Analysis* (pp. 108–144). Chicago: University of Chicago Press.

Simpson, M., & Cheney, G. (2007). Marketization, participation, and communication within New Zealand retirement villages: A critical–rhetorical and discursive analysis. *Discourse & Communication*, *1*, 191–222.

Skelcher, C., & Smith, S. R. (2015). Theorizing hybridity: Institutional logics, complex organisations, and actor identities: The case of nonprofits. *Public Administration*, *93*(2), 433–448.

Smets, M., Jarzabkowski, P., Burke, G., & Spee, P. (2015). Reinsurance trading in Lloyd's of London: Balancing conflicting-yet-complementary logics in practice. *Academy of Management Journal*, *58*, 932–970.

Smith, S. R. (2014). Hybridity and Nonprofit Organizations: The research agenda. *American Behavioral Scientist*, *58*(11), 1494–1508.

Stryker, S., & Burke, P. (2000). The past, present, and future of an identity theory. *Social Psychology Quarterly*, *63*(4), 284–297.

Suchman, M. (1995). Managing legitimacy: strategic and institutional approaches. *The Academy of Management Review*, *20*(3).

Tassie, B., Murray, V., & Cutt, J. (1998). Evaluating social service agencies: Fuzzy pictures of organizational effectiveness. *Voluntas: International Journal of Voluntary and Nonprofit Organizations*, *9*(1), 59–79.

Terry, L. D. (1998). Administrative leadership, neo-managerialism, and the public management movement. *Public Administration Review* *58*(3), 194–200.

Thornton, P., Ocasio, W., & Lounsbury, M. (2012). *Institutional Logics Perspective: A New Appraoch to Culture, Structure and Process* (1st ed.). USA: Oxford University Press.

Tilcsik, A. (2010). From ritual to reality: Demography, idelogy and docoupling in post-communist government agency. *Academy of Management Journal*, 6, 1474–1498.

Tilly, C. (2005). *Social Movements, 1768–2004*, Boulder CO: Paradigm Publishers.

Turco, C. (2012). Difficult decoupling: Employee resistence to the commercialization of personal settings. *American Journal of Sociology*, *118*(2), 380–419.

Van Maanen J. (1989) *Tales of the field: On writing ethnography*. Chicago: University of Chicago Press.

Van Maanen, J. (2011). Ethnography as work: some rules of engagement. *Journal of Management Studies*, *48*, 218–234.

Watson, T. J. (2001). *In Search of Management: Culture, Chaos and Control in Managerial Work*. Revised Edition. London: Thomson Learning.

Weick, K. E. (2002). Real-time reflexivity, prods to reflection. *Organizational Studies*, *23*(6), 893–898.

Weick, K. E. (1993). The collapse of sensemaking in organizations: The Mann Gulch disaster. *Administrative Science Quarterly*, *38*, 628–652.

Weick, K. E. (1989). Theory construction as disciplined imagination. *The Academy of Management Review*, *14*(4), 516–531.

Weisbrod, Burton A. (Ed.) (1998). *To Profit or Not to Profit: The Commercial Transformation of the Nonprofit Sector*. Cambridge, UK: Cambridge University Press.

Westphal, J., & Zajac. (1999). Co-operative or controlling: The effects of CEO–Board relations and the content of interlocks on the formation of joint ventures. *Administrative Science Quarterly*, *44*(3), 473–506.

Wolch, J. R. (1990). *The shadow state: Government and voluntary sector in transition*. New York: The Foundation Center.

Yanow, D., & Geuijen, K. (2009). Annotated bibliography: Defining "organizational ethnography": Selection criteria. In S. Ybema, D. Yanow, H. Wels, & F. Kamsteeg (Eds), *Organizational ethnography: Studying the complexities of everyday life* (pp. 253–259). London, UK: Sage

Zilber, T. (2002). Institutionalization as an interplay between actions, meanings and actors: The case of a rape crisis centre in Israel. *Academy of Management Journal*, *45*, 234–254.

Part I

A Tale of Two Rhetorics

Organizational Life in the Milieu of Corporate and Community Logics

Part I of the book looks at the hybrid world of the association by exploring inhabitants' struggles to make sense of organizational purpose in the face of divergent organizing logics, the contested, political nature of managerial work within this milieu and the role of symbolism, rhetoric and strategizing in rewriting the organization's script.

2 An Organization in Search of Purpose

"The challenges faced by us as a nonprofit organization are considerable and tensions between making a sustainable income and staying true to the mission are inevitable. We recognise and embrace the rival metaphors of (social) mission and business; our driver remains to make money to do more things to deliver to our public good agenda."

(Strategy Document, incumbent CEO)

A Short Version of a Long History

The emergence of the association began in the early part of the 20th century, forming into a British Association with a constitution, membership fees and an initial general meeting in the 1930s. At this time, the association consisted of 100 members of the profession it existed to serve. Between 1940 and 1970, the association introduced elements of an education scheme followed by specialist education programmes, commenced publication of a journal, held an annual dinner and national conference, and began engaging with issues of international importance to the profession. Membership reached circa 5000 and special interest groups and membership branches reached 43 across the U.K. and overseas.

During the 1970s, increasing the profile of the association and the profession took on greater emphasis and the decision was made to try and achieve Royal Charter status. With this status came a focus on degree-level education programmes, membership levels linked to educational and professional achievement and development of a code of ethics by which all members were bound. Membership rose to over 17,000, with high growth in overseas members as global companies sought to get staff qualified by the profession's chartered body. The objects of the Charter included: promoting and developing the art and science (including improving methods) of the profession for public benefit; promoting and maintaining standards of skill, ability and integrity for public benefit; educating and assessing skills and knowledge of individuals entering the profession and the association. Alongside Charter status, the association registered as an education charity.

The association's first 3-year strategy was produced and approved in the mid-1990s; it aimed to grow membership, knowledge development and qualifications and included measures of effectiveness against Charter objects. A large Trustee body of almost 50 provided oversight of progress. Each Trustee had to be a member of the association through completion of the degree-level education programme and display a high level of professional standing. A decade later, the first CEO from the profession and from a background solely in large corporates was recruited. This, in my experience, heralded the managerialization and commercialization of the association. So, what did this entail? In essence, as we will explore in later chapters, structural change through the creation of charitable and corporate subsidiaries, an overhaul of governance structures and processes, re-imagining performance criteria, evolving recruitment, reward and recognition practices and a very different sense of "what it feels like to work around here." From a growth perspective, the transformation was undeniably successful, resulting in over 65,000 members in 150 countries, over 70,000 assessments/examinations undertaken per annum, a £25 million annual turnover and around 150 staff. What was less clear, was whom and for what purpose all this growth was ultimately for. A senior colleague, who had spent 25 years in the association, provided the following account of the organization's trajectory in an email correspondence:

> "The balance between the competing tracks of public benefit and commercial success is fluid and changes over time. We have moved from being focused on membership and education with members as our primary customers in the 1990s – when we had just got our charter and did virtually no marketing or PR (Public Relations) activity (because advertising was a dirty word for a chartered professional body) and did very little promotion to organisational customers – to one where corporate revenue has become king and we are now actually pleased that we are reducing our reliance on qualifications and membership fees as a source of revenue, which we now see as a potential source of vulnerability. It seems to me there have been three main reasons for that change:
>
> a Success in the Charter application was wholly dependent on presenting a convincing message on public good. Everything we did at that time was geared towards orienting the institute towards the public good agenda, the submission to the Privy Council was wholly predicated on justifying our credentials as a public interest body. Financial success was only a factor in that it was the fuel to support sustainability and corporates were only important because they paid for exams and fees. The Privy Council looks for evidence that the new Chartered body is

financially stable and will remain a going concern, but otherwise has no interest in how much money we make. We repeated the public good mantra so often at the time it became our mythology. This imperative characterised the launch of the new Chartered body and influenced its culture for more than a decade thereafter.

b The Spada (2009) report on UK professional bodies and the CCPMO (Consultative Committee for Professional Management Organisations) report (earlier, can't recall the date) into the value-add of professional bodies both identified that the professional landscape was changing dramatically and no professional body could assume it had a right to exist just because it had been around for years and claimed to serve the public good. Bodies had to stay relevant, be more commercial and sell themselves to their stakeholders. So, the move towards a more commercial mind-set was a necessity, a long-term survival strategy. There was a general movement in the professional body world over the last decade to become more business-like in response to the threat of losing relevance, so it has been a defensive move to some extent.

c The third factor has been the professionalization of [the association] itself. When I joined, most senior posts (other than the educationalists) were held by retired service personnel or others who had moved out of London and were looking for a quiet wind-down to retirement. Very few members of staff had Masters degrees or professional qualifications. Crucially, until around 1997 the CEOs of the institute were non-business people, they were interested in the professional body but not the business per se. My perception is that it is only really since 1997 when we started to have CEOs with commercial backgrounds and we started to employ managers with business qualifications and private sector backgrounds that the multiple identities of [the association] has really become apparent."

Within this book we primarily focus on organizational life during the incumbent CEO's term of office, at times holding it in tension with the former CEO's approach for purposes of comparison. Their proffered organizing logics stand in sharp contrast, raising the question of how one CEO can bring about such a transformational shift within an organization that has such a long history and deeply embedded social purpose script. As a director of the association with over 14 years' service prior to "going researcher," my belief is that there was a critical juncture that provided the context for or facilitated the organization's shift from its historical trajectory.

The incumbent CEO's entry into the association came after a lengthy period of stability and moderate growth under the former long-term CEO. There was, however, an intervening period with a CEO from a nonprofit, professional association background, who was removed by the board of trustees after only a short time. The narrative around their removal related to poor financial decisions that had dramatically reduced the association's financial reserves. At that moment, the soon-to-be-incumbent CEO was on the board of trustees and, as the story goes, seized the opportunity to create a "burning platform" around the financial state of the association. The argument was that such low reserves contravened charity "best practice" and that there was an urgent need to address the situation through appointing someone with a "business" background to turn the institute around, while at the same time "throwing their hat in the ring." The board of trustees appointed them on a 3-year fixed-term contract based on a manifesto of securing a strong, stable financial position for the association. This was the first time a CEO of the association had been on a fixed-term contract. Presumably, this was a conscious signal that the CEO's manifesto, and therefore the CEO, would become redundant once sufficient reserves were rebuilt. As we show in Chapter 4, this CEO skilfully placed the association as perpetually under threat (from competitors, from the global financial crisis, etc.), necessitating a sustained focus on commerciality. Private negotiations with the Chair of the board resulted in the CEO acquiring a permanent employment contract and at some point, most people stopped asking why or for what purpose we needed more and more "profit."

The Logic of Nonprofit Organization: Making Sense of Hybridity

As an institute incorporated by Royal Charter, a registered charity and an increasingly commercial entity, the association was an archetypal hybrid organization, balancing multiple regulatory regimes and cultural logics (Kraatz & Block, 2008). It was pluralistic in respect of divergent goals, interests, identities and purposes yet increasingly hierarchical and I, for one, was experiencing a war between the "rival metaphors" of "mission and business." Through the politics of everyday life, changes in CEO and board membership, development of new organizational structures, a new and intense emphasis on contracting, commercial relationships and operational efficiencies, the association felt like it was in transition. There were observable processes of negotiation and persuasion, formation and reformation of coalitions and interactions between people that seemed to create or undermine patterns of thought and behaviour based on allegiance to either "the mission" (and a community logic) or "the business" (and a corporate logic). As a member of the senior leadership team, there were many times I asked myself "is it just me? Are others experiencing tensions and seemingly incoherent sets of beliefs, assumptions and messages or am I simply struggling with the change in CEO and a new 'social order?'" This, it seemed, had to be the starting point for my research. In separate conversations, two colleagues put it this way:

> "… Some people think, 'oh, we have to make sure we're doing right for the charity,' and then there's another group in the middle who are like 'oh, we can be commercial and be charitable; why don't people get that?' And they get kind of defensive around what they're doing and people judging them to be wholly commercial. And then I think there's another group which are about 'my job is to be commercial, I have a target to hit, I'll let the others worry about the need to be charitable.' So, yeah, I think the tension is between those who want to be commercial, those who are commercial but see themselves as being commercial in the 'right way' versus those who … recognise the organisation is a charity and that's their first port of call." [Director]

> "I think perceptions of [the association] as charitable or commercial or both depend almost entirely on where a person sits in the organization and what their KPIs are – bearing in mind that people who have been here longer tend to be more resistant to moving towards a commercial model because they have the corporate memory from the award of Charter. The face of [the association] that you first see and interact with forms your worldview. When you think about it, everyone should wear both hats but if you drew a spectrum from charity to commercial enterprise and asked everyone to a) mark where on the line they think [the association] sits and b) where on the line they think their job sits, there would be a wide variation in where all the dots were." [Senior Manager]

What became apparent very quickly in my conversations with colleagues was that they frame and make sense of the organization and its purpose in multiple and divergent ways. By framing, we are referring to the ways in which people create a "schemata of interpretation" (Goffman, 1974, p. 21) to discursively reconfigure boundaries, sometimes in a contest-like fashion, or invoke new understandings in the process of sensemaking (see Sewell, 1992; Lounsbury et al., 2003; Werner & Cornelissen, 2014; Bucher et al., 2016). Figure 2.1 pictorially represents four framings of the association presented in everyday talk; two that we associate with a community logic (Frames A and B) and two we suggest are underpinned by a corporate logic (Frames C and D).

Frame A – Charter

Charter status acted as a reference point for some individuals to make sense of the organization and its purpose, but this tended to be for people who had been at the organization for a long time, and was certainly not the narrative of the majority. The former CEO commented:

> "[The association] has got a Royal Charter, it's there to do public good and it explains in the Royal Charter the four ways it's

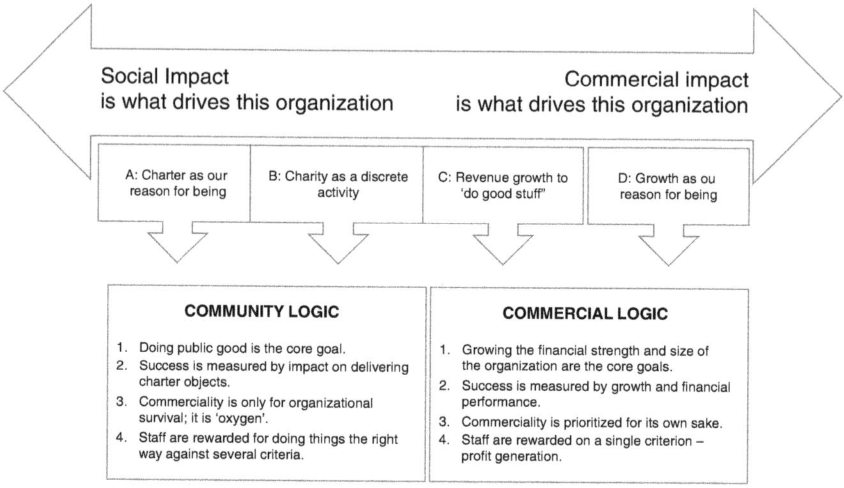

Figure 2.1 Framing the organization and its purpose.
Source: Bain (2017).

> supposed to do it. So, it's not difficult to define what the purpose of the organization is if people decide they want to have a look. It's very simple. There are four things I used to say. It's about helping individuals, helping organizations, representing the profession, and developing improved methods."

As someone who had experienced organizational life under the term of this CEO, it was clear to me that the Charter had acted to guide their articulation of the association's purpose, how that purpose should be achieved and the norms and practices that had taken hold as a result. It was also my sense that the Charter was increasingly absented in current decision-making processes.

Frame B – Charity

Constituting the association as a charity was also rare within the organization, despite its legal status as a registered charity. A trustee who had previous experience of working in charities evoked the strongest depiction of the association as a charity, stating "I don't see it as a business. I see it as a charity that needs to generate income in order to deliver its core purpose. If it wants to be a training company, then it should not have charitable status." Sceptics felt that "we have charitable status because it gives an exemption to corporation tax" [Director] and a charity identity was something we "pick up and put down when it suits us" [Middle Manager].

Others positioned "charity" as something we "do" rather than something we "are." Charity, in many colleagues' eyes, was decoupled from the association's core activity and was undertaken through a subsidiary charity with separate governance structures and processes. This was seen as "a small part of what we do" [Senior Manager] or the "corporate social responsibility arm of [the association] … kind of like a side arm" [Middle Manager]. A fellow Director surmised:

> "There are a lot of people within the organization … [who] don't actually appreciate we're a charity. What that actually means, they certainly won't understand the public good piece and they just think that we're there as any other commercial organization to, you know, survive and thrive; make loads and loads of money."

Frame C – Hybrid

A sizeable group of people simultaneously constitute the association around two organizing principles shared by Frame A (Charter) and Frame D (Commercial). This framing shares with the Charter frame the sentiment that the organization's purpose is to enhance and represent the profession. What is notably different, however, is a far greater acceptance of the prioritization of making money, but there were conditions to the acceptance of commerciality as one colleague points out:

> "We need to be commercially focused. However, it's about maybe not being too commercial. We need to be aware of who we are and what we stand for and not forget that." [Middle Manager]

Among this group there is a deeply entrenched rhetoric of making money "to put to good use," "to do more things," and "to do good stuff," but in a departure from the Charity and Charter frames, actors constructing this particular framing never made explicit the nature of these social goods.

Frame D – Commercial

Proponents of this frame position commerciality as a legitimate organizational driver in its own right. As one colleague put it, the common, identifiable threads relate to "global presence; being the biggest and the best; making [the association] more and more unassailable." [Senior Manager]. Another described achievement of profit targets – now the principal measure of success or key performance indicator – as a "self-preservation thing" [Graduate Programme] given its centrality to the incumbent CEO's agenda:

> " … CEO's ethos is to make loads and loads of money, yeah, but [CEO] doesn't necessarily want to do things with it. They want to

> basically, it's a horrible phrase, but to hoard it and basically make [the association] a lot more financially stable than it is. So, they want to accumulate, you know, a reserve, cash reserves and all the rest of it, but ultimately, that's not there to do things; that's just to make us more financially secure." [Director]

In sum, the association was simultaneously constituted by corporate and community logics, where competing frames infiltrate organizational life and sensemaking processes. Within the framings listed earlier we can observe the use of words, ideas and values anchored in particular cultural background knowledge and latent meaning structures that suggest how practices or boundaries in respect of organizational purpose can be (re)considered (Goffman, 1974; Suddaby & Greenwood, 2005). In other words, organizational inhabitants draw on common cultural frames of reference as to how things *should* be done as normative resources in their framings of the association. We now narrate what this means for the negotiation of organizational means and ends.

Getting Down to Basics: Negotiating Means and Ends

In Aristotelian ethics, economics *(oikenomia)* and business is systematically connected to a moral and political philosophy (Dierksmeier & Pirson, 2009). For Aristotle, economics is the allocation of resources towards the pursuit of happiness or human flourishing in the form of a well-ordered life and society *(eudaemonia)*. Whereas money represents an instrumental means to happiness if it is utilised well, the pursuit of money or profit for its own sake *(chrematistics)* is an irrational or unnatural activity as it dehumanizes those who participate in it; it leads to imbalance and excess because it is inherently limitless (Aristotle *et al.*, 1980). Such a philosophy would seem generally coherent with the emergence and espoused ideals and purpose of nonprofit organizing.

Within the association, the multiple and sometimes overlapping framings of organizational purpose create ambiguity in what are taken to be the means and ends of organizational activities (see Figure 2.2). For some, commerciality is merely the means to achieve public good (sharing parallels with eudaemonia). For others money and growth has become the end game itself (chrematistics). Over my time at the association, it seemed that the former had become a marginalized view with the latter increasingly taking center stage.

A Community Logic

The increasingly marginalized charity and charter frames imply an overarching logic of community; positive social impact is the raison d'être or the "end" it exists to achieve. This rests upon service to a particular professional

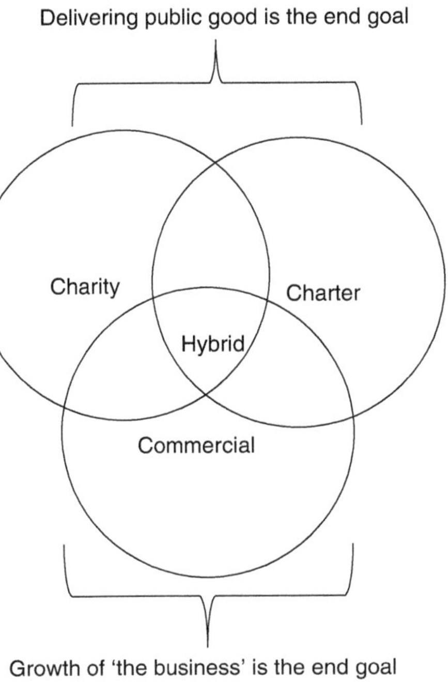

Figure 2.2 Framing and organizational ends.

community of practice, decision-making is driven explicitly by (perceived) contribution to public good and performance measurement takes account of not just what we achieve, but how we achieve it. Making money is a necessity; it serves as oxygen to enable the organization to meet Charter objectives and thus public good. It is a route or means to *eudaemonia*.

The former CEO's inherent belief was that "if we do the right thing [by the profession], the money will follow." This had served him and the association well, leading to a secure financial position and surpluses that were re-invested into developing additional services for the benefit of the professional community:

> "Financially, we exceeded budget in the first two years of the [3-year strategic] plan and a similar surplus is forecast for the current FY [financial year]. This enabled us to invest in developing new products and services as we had planned and to build our reserves for investment in the [next] plan. The additional revenue growth resulted from a greater volume of engagements with individuals and organisations in combination with price increases in some areas. We aim to continue this upward trend to generate significant surpluses over each of the [next] three years, which we will then

use to fund the plan and achieve our objectives. Revenue will continue to grow incrementally. However, the plan includes a step function increase in ongoing costs in year one, including an extra ten staff members (to deliver more knowledge, marketing/PR and start to build sales processes), and overheads (additional office space). There will also be some one-off costs in year one in relation to the handover to the new CEO. This results in the surplus falling back in [year 1]. As revenue continues to grow, however, the surplus will increase again in two consecutive FYs. Project spend will be managed in relation to the surplus generated and will be focused on key areas of impact."

(3-Year Strategy, written by former CEO)

In management meetings, Charter objects served as the central organizing principle – a touchstone for strategic conversations and decision-making. During the former CEO's term of office, the organization was a registered charity delivering activities deemed to have a positive social impact for the association's membership-base and wider profession, thereby delivering to the Charter. In this sense, there was a recursive relationship between the means and ends of the association (see Figure 2.3).

The interpretation of the Charter objects into a vision and mission for the organization provides insight into divergent organizing logics, and this is something we will come back to in the subsequent sub-section. The former CEO advanced the following articulation of vision and mission within his strategic plan:

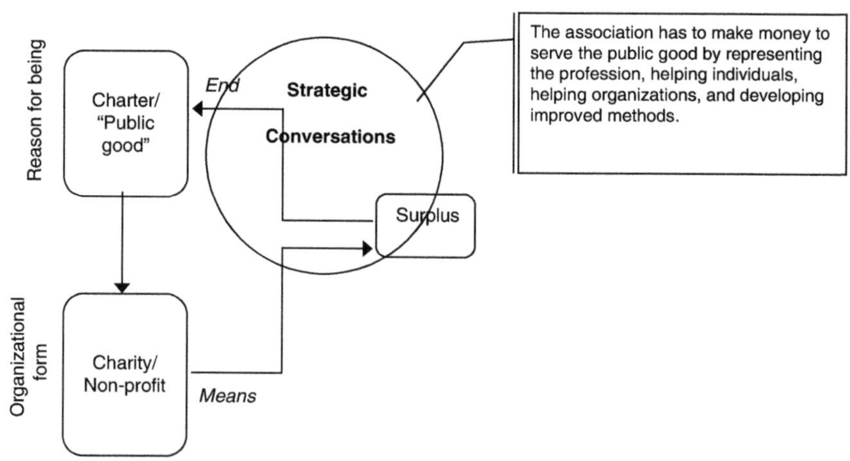

Figure 2.3 Organizational means and ends within a community logic.
Source: Adapted from Bain (2017).

"Vision: We will achieve universal recognition that excellence in [function] is an imperative for responsible organisational success and hence the public good."

Mission: "The Institute will fulfil the objectives of its Royal Charter, deliver value to its stakeholders and be recognised as a point of reference and authority. Specifically, it will:

- Promote, represent and explain the business discipline and good practice of [function].
- Research, develop and endorse improved methods in [function].
- Assist all organisations in developing their capability in [function] with the right strategies, processes, people and leadership.
- Support individuals in developing, demonstrating and qualifying in the profession."

A corporate logic

The hybrid and commercial frames constitute a corporate logic, privileging a growthist agenda in terms of global presence, financial and human resources. Increasing "profit" is the end goal; being a charity and chartered organization is now a means to that end through utilizing associated notions of impartiality, ethics and quality for competitive advantage. Revenue, profit growth and the ability to share (financial) success with staff become the main drivers for decision-making and organizational activity. True to the goal of chrematistics, performance and "wealth" are measured only in (the unlimited accumulation of) money; a powerful tool in closing down discussions of wider social responsibility (Miller & Power, 2013).

In management team meetings during the incumbent CEO's term, strategic discussions were focused on the impact of decisions on growing profit and strengthening the organization's "war chest." At the start of this CEO's term in the late 2000s financial sustainability came into sharper focus within formal strategic plans (see first quote), which intensified to the point of demanding surplus financial "profits" 4 years later (see second quote):

> "To meet these challenges [the association] has to change to ensure we are fit for purpose ... We are dependent on three principal revenue streams ... Our aim is to maintain these three revenue streams in broad balance to mitigate against any sudden changes."

> "Within the next three years it is planned that total sales will reach £30m; over double where they were [when I started] and representing consistently strong year-on-year growth. Profit and Loss centres will be targeted to be profitable at net financial return (NFR) level in next FY to counter the fall in [product] contribution as we move to a new segmented customized offering. Essential to our on-going growth is stronger cash reserves, which will be driven by targeting a minimum of £1m cash, returned to reserves from [x]FY onwards. Underpinning this will be an improving return on sales to 8% and balancing debtor/creditor days at 45 days each average. This will allow us to actively address the pension deficit and build a 'war chest' for potential acquisitions."

The association became "the business" in everyday talk and increasing the association's financial strength and size is positioned, in its own right, as a justifiable way to deliver public good. The charter serves as the means to economic or financial ends (see Figure 2.4).

Revisiting the interpretation of vision and mission, in contrast to the former CEO's emphasis on public good, responsible organization and management and delivering value to stakeholders, the incumbent CEO honed in sharply on being the leading, global authority; competition and competitiveness, and; being the first port of call:

> "**Vision:** To be the authority that is leading global excellence in [function].

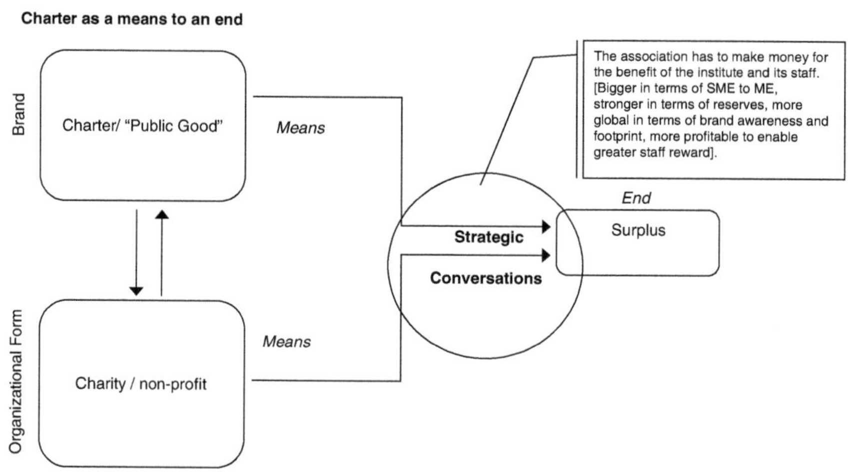

Figure 2.4 Organizational means and ends within a corporate logic.
Source: Adapted from Bain (2017).

Within this mission we have recognised there will be others with similar aspirations but we believe that we already have a unique global community from which we can launch and the beginnings of authority status in the eyes of many. Much more will be needed to develop this but if we do not, others will. Given we currently focus on the U.K., maintenance of that base will be vital as, at least initially, it will fund our global aspirations.

"We will seek to build our current product portfolio into global and regional products operating through our regional centres with significant investment in digital technology. A new global structure with regional hubs will seek to strengthen our global presence whilst not diluting precious resources."

Mission: Through the delivery of this Strategic Plan, the [association] will become recogniszd as *the global standard and authority* for the licensing of [function] professionals. This will include being the global reference point for knowledge and custodian of the standards. We will be working in partnership with all forms of organization and government to achieve our global position. Our systems, people and brand will be developed to achieve this global status.

A new mechanism to achieve this will be the concept of [new strategic development], both for corporate learning and also to attract the best to the profession through Masters level qualifications and awards. This will underpin our key ambition to gain 'Licence' status for the profession.

"Our core theme of [name removed] encapsulates our intent to be the automatic first port of call for [function] professionals, a signpost to the latest knowledge, tools and techniques and best practice."

What is notable about the different CEOs' articulation of the vision and mission is that they both speak to notions of achieving universal or global excellence and establishing the association as a point of reference or authority for the profession. Within the community logic, however, this is the means for creating "higher" ends such as responsible management practices, delivering value to stakeholders and public good itself. Within the corporate organizing logic, being seen as "the authority that is leading global excellence" is the means to beat the competition; to be the first, the biggest and the best. In essence, the new CEO was re-writing the organizational script (discussed further in Chapter 4). A long-term colleague and senior manager in the association provided the following reflection after I shared some early findings from the field:

> "Looking at the kind of language your respondents have used to describe 'doing more things,' I recognise the difficulty people have once you get beyond a certain point in the argument. It is very difficult for anyone to identify a specific, quantifiable, public good outcome. The language gets fuzzy and imprecise. The problem is that the reinvestment model is circular and virtually perpetual – we have never arrived at the end. So, we earn money and then invest it in activities which generate more money which in turn we invest in more activities that earn more money, and so on ... [This] creates a self-fulfilling pattern of corporate behaviour to which it is almost impossible to say 'stop.'"

This struck a chord with me, reminding me of an experience at an all-staff away day. Part of the day was dedicated to creating a film about the association, which could be used for the induction of new staff. We were allocated to groups of around 6–8 people and my group happened to include the CEO. Much of the event is hazy to me – I generally get quite traumatized by role-play – but I recall the CEO's analogy of their role as akin to the captain of a ship, and that they wore a captain's hat. My main memory is that at the end of each "scene," the camera cut to the CEO who shouted the words "More, more, more; I want more" while holding up a fistful of bank notes. When our group's film was shown to the audience (the entire staff group), the room reacted with a mixture of laughter from some sections and looks of horror from others. The final image cut to a close-up headshot of me silently mouthing the words "what the fuck." This captured not only my thoughts of "what am I doing here?" but was also a reaction to the CEO's demands for "more, more, more." I had not intended my reaction to be captured on film and am known for keeping my emotions off my face at work, but on this occasion the veil slipped.

Though the pursuit of profit maximization is largely alien in the context of many social purpose organizations, modern business theory from the neo-classical economic paradigm "has established a moral code of business based on efficiency of outcome and the assumed link of efficiency to self-interested behaviour," resulting in "markets as the arbitrators of ethical outcomes, and profit maximization as the ultimate moral code" (Keller, 2007, p. 159). For carriers of a corporate logic, such as the incumbent CEO, profit maximization remains the ultimate moral code, regardless of the organizational context they now inhabit and reinvent. Within the association, the (re)conception of organizational means and ends, or re-writing of the organizational script, intensified managerialism and commercialization to the point of transforming its trajectory away from the original (social) purpose. Table 2.1 summarizes the core features of the organizing logics across various aspects of organizing, which will be elaborated over the course of the book.

Table 2.1 Features of the community and corporate logics constituting the association

	Community Logic	*Corporate Logic*
Identity	Based on emotional connections, ego-satisfaction and reputation	Based on bureaucratic roles
Authority	Based on personal investment, commitment to shared values and ideology	Based on status in hierarchy (board/top management)
Legitimacy	Comes from achieving a state of unity in deciding what is desirable, based on trust and reciprocity	Comes from market position of the business
Strategy	Increase (organizational and societal) status of associational members, wider profession and their practices through cooperation	Increase size and diversification of business through competition
Norms	Developed through associational membership (of staff/profession groups)	Developed through employment relationship with the business
Informal control mechanism	Through visibility of actions; doing the "right" things, in the "right" way	Through strong organizational culture

Source: adapted from Thornton et al., 2012.

References

Aristotle., Ross, W. D., Urmson, J. O., & Ackrill, J. L. (1980). *The Nicomachean ethics*. Oxford: Oxford University Press.

Bain, C. (2017). *Interplay of Intentions: An Ethnography of Institutional Work Within a Hybrid Organization*. Unpublished DBA Thesis. Sheffield, UK: Sheffield Hallam University.

Bucher, S. V., Chreim, S., Langley, A., & Reay, T. (2016). Contestation about collaboration: Discursive boundary work among professions. *Organization Studies*, *37*(4), 497–522.

Chapman, J., Conlon, G., & Muller, P. (2008). *An Economic Impact Assessment of the CCPMO (Consultative Committee for Professional Management Organisations)*. London: London Economics.

Dierksmeier, C., & Pirson, M. (2009). Oikonomia and Chrematistike, Learning from Aristotle About the Future of Management. *Journal of Business Ethics*, *88*(3), 417–430.

Goffman, E. (1974). *Frame Analysis: An Essay on the Organization of Experience*. Boston, MA: North Eastern University Press.

Keller, A. C. (2007). Smith versus Friedman: Markets and ethics. *Critical Perspectives on Accounting*, *18*(2), 159–188.

Kraatz, M. S., & Block, E. S. (2008). Organizational implications of institutional pluralism. In R. Greenwood, C. Oliver, K. Sahlin-Andersson & R. Suddaby (Eds), *The SAGE Handbook of Organizational Institutionalism* (pp. 243–275). Thousand Oaks, CA: SAGE.

Lounsbury, M., Ventresca, P., & Hirsch, M. (2003). Social movements, field frames and industry emergence: A cultural–political perspective on US recycling. *Socio-Economic Review*, *1*(1), 71–104.

Miller, P., & Power, M. (2013). Accounting, organizing, and economizing: Connecting accounting research and organization theory. *Academy of Management Annals*, *7*(1), 557–605.

Sewell, W. H. (1992). A theory of structure: Duality, agency and transformation. *American Journal of Sociology*, *98*(1), 1–29.

Spada. (2009). *British Professions Today: The State of the Sector*. London: Spada.

Suddaby, R., & Greenwood, R. (2005). Rhetorical strategies of legitimacy. *Administrative Science Quarterly*, *50*(1), 35–67.

Thornton, P., Ocasio, W., & Lounsbury, M. (2012). *Institutional Logics Perspective: A New Appraoch to Culture, Structure and Process* (1st ed.) USA: Oxford University Press.

Werner, M. D., & Cornelissen, J. P. (2014). Framing the change: Switching blending frames and their role in instigating institutional change. *Organization Studies*, *35*(10), 1449–1472.

3 Managers in Search of Purpose

Senior Manager:	"In a sense, Mariella is the owner of the kind of regulatory side. In fact, there's a great responsibility on her. We always hear they could go to prison."
Carole:	"Can I just check that you are saying that you have been told that if someone does something that didn't meet regulatory standards, Mariella would go to prison?"
Senior Manager:	"That's the ultimate message we get given. That's the end story, but yes, I mean it's the one thing we all fear. We would hate to put her in prison. That would be a nightmare, wouldn't it? [Laughs] But no, we'd hate to have [the regulator] coming down on us and putting serious financial penalties in as well."

Drawing the Battle Lines: Heroes and Villains

The multiple logics within the association produce contradictions that managers use to draw battle lines between (social) "good" and (economic) "evil" within the organization. Within my day-to-day work I became aware of emotionally charged conversations between two departments led by different directors for whom we use the pseudonyms Mariella and Geoff. Mariella's department was responsible for promoting and protecting standards within the association and the profession; Geoff's was responsible for corporate activity, or more specifically delivering educational products to corporate entities. From the outset, their respective job descriptions and role expectations set the two directors and the functions they oversee on a course to work against each other (see Table 3.1).

Table 3.1 Director-level job description comparison

Job Summary	
Mariella	*Geoff*
A1. Responsible for the development and continuous improvement of global education standards that meet regulatory and market needs and position [the association] as the leading authority and standard setter for the profession.	B1. Accountability for the delivery of all B2B products and services, maintaining margins leading to increased returns (financial and volume).
Key Responsibilities [in order of presentation on Job Description]	
A2. Develop, manage and deliver a global plan that promotes and adheres to professional standards.	B2. Input into the Corporate Strategy and business Plans, with responsibility and accountability for the delivery of corporate products and services, maintaining margin and maximising financial return.
A3. Develop, manage, deliver and maintain the *[name]* International Standard ensuring that it meets the needs of global markets and supports the Public Benefit needs of the Charter.	B3. Lead and direct Group Product Development activities, developing new leading edge products and enhancing current offerings to maximise profit and increase market penetration and reputation.
A4. Develop, manage and deliver new global education products and services that will support and continuously raise standards and meet the needs of the corporate market.	B4. Lead and direct the maintenance and expansion of local and international senior professional networks (member and non-member), Corporate and individual stakeholder groups to support reputational growth and influence and exploit business opportunities.

A5.	Lead and direct the continuous development of educational/ assessed programmes to meet current and future market needs – both in the academic world to ensure world-class status and to meet the needs of the corporate market.	B5.	Lead and direct key/strategic supplier networks to ensure continued quality of delivery and availability of a range of appropriate partners to meet current and future demand.
A6.	Lead and direct alternative routes to membership ensuring no detriment to standards of entry.	B6.	Control and manage the department's finances to ensure effective budgeting and cost control.
A7.	Lead and direct the management and continuous improvement of a range of academic consultants/providers to ensure on-time, quality provision of examination material, coupled with robust marking and assessment to agreed standards.	B7.	Direct and develop staff of the department to ensure they are appropriately motivated, trained and are working towards the achievement of plans and objectives.
A8.	Lead, direct and protect the independence of the Awarding Body, ensuring strong compliance, clarity of purposes and continuous improvement.		*End of Document*
A9.	Responsible and accountable for protecting the legally binding regulatory compliance status of the Awarding Body.		
A10.	Lead representative/ambassador in the global education arena and wider into the corporate market to support reputational and business growth.		
A11.	Responsible and accountable for the provision and continuous maintenance and growth of a global network of education providers, ensuring fairness, open access and formal auditing to maintain standards and to meet the Charter objectives of 'access for all'.		

(*Continued*)

Table 3.1 (*Continued*)

Job Summary	
Mariella	*Geoff*
A12. Responsible and accountable for assessment methodologies to support the currency and credibility of the global standard and lead current thinking in the academic world and to ensure relevance to other stakeholders.	
A13. Responsible and accountable for the continuous monitoring of Government, agencies and other global educational bodies to assess potential impact and opportunities for professional development activities.	
A14. Control and manage the department's finances to ensure effective budgeting and cost control.	
A15. Direct and develop the staff of the department to ensure that they are appropriately motivated, trained and are working towards the achievement of business plans.	

Source: Bain (2017).

As context, the role holders had each drafted their own job description for approval by the CEO, with the Human Resources (HR) department then adding standardized items relating to people and budget management (A14 and A15; B6 and B7). Mariella had worked in several regulated environments in a number of different organizations. This had mostly been within education, and in small–medium sized charities and nonprofit organizations. Geoff had worked for 25 years prior to joining the association in privately owned large corporate organizations; this is his first charity and first small–medium sized organization.

There are a number of important points to note. First, Mariella's role walks the "hybrid" line between commerciality and public good. The role description pays homage to addressing market needs [A1, A3, A4, A5, A10], but constantly positions it next to maintaining and improving standards and reputation, meeting regulatory requirements and achieving Charter objectives and public benefit. In stark contrast, Geoff's role is devoid of (nonprofit) organizational context, focusing solely on maximization of financial returns [B1, B2, B3, B4]. Second, the descriptors stand in opposition at a rhetorical level, with Mariella positioned as the "protector" of standards, fairness, open access and ultimately Charter objectives [A6, A8, A9, A11] and Geoff as the "exploiter" of business opportunities for greater market penetration [B3, B4]. A community logic, where addressing market needs is the means to achieving a higher social purpose, is inherent in Mariella's articulation of her role. For Geoff, making money is the end game itself. Such competing organizing principles can inevitably set managers, functions and departments at war with each other based on allegiance to one logic or another. That the directors had each been socialized throughout their professional life with divergent logics, which they subsequently bring to the fore in constructing their job roles, supports the idea of employees as "carriers" of institutional logics (Greenwood & Hinings, 1993; Zilber, 2002). This is not to suggest that they are mere cultural dopes, simply acting out the directives provided by cultural, organizational and societal norms to which they have been exposed (Garfinkle, 1967; Tolbert & Zucker, 1996). As we will see in this chapter, organizational inhabitants are artful and agentic in exploiting the ambiguities and contradictions inherent in hybrid organizations towards their own ends, not least through creating and deploying "rational(ized) myths" (Meyer & Rowan, 1977; Zilber, 2006; Bayma, 2012).

At a broader level, the two directors' respective departments were operating under different principles or regimes. Mariella's department, and its associated "education" profit and loss account, was expected to break even whereas Geoff's "corporate" profit and loss account was expected to generate over half of the £1 million per annum return to financial reserves target. Mariella had actively and successfully fended off the intensified pressure for income and growth outlined in Chapter 2 by citing the regulator's interest in ensuring participation and accessibility to education as a significant risk to the association's awarding body status (and associated revenue) should prices increase too greatly. This was strengthened by an imminent routine audit by the regulator. Mariella's department was achieving a break-even position with income being sufficient to cover its cost base. Geoff's department, however, was making a loss and a "CEO Task Force" to secure profitability was initiated. At a senior leadership team meeting a few months later, Geoff presented the Task Force as the "Keeping me in a job project," using serious humor to express a level of concern around personal consequences. For me, this brought context to the shock I had felt at a previous meeting when Geoff suggested it would be beneficial if learners failed their exams, as they would then transfer onto a new programme giving greater financial returns.

One incident in particular is useful in illustrating the internal battles that can arise in the milieu of divergent organizing logics. The incident involved Mariella challenging Geoff over a marketing email promoting one of his team's new educational products. Mariella felt that Geoff had used privileged access to internal data in an unfair way and to the detriment of external stakeholders (namely, other study centers that delivered the association's qualifications). Mariella claimed that Geoff's team was not authorized to access or use her team's data, that this constituted a conflict of interest and that by using it Geoff and his team had compromised the integrity of the Awarding Body. Ultimately, she argued, this put the association at risk of regulatory action. I experienced much persuasive and emotive rhetoric around this incident from both parties, as Mariella and her department appropriate a "protector of public good" identity as a justification for policing and sanctioning other functions within the organization.

Internal Policing, Sanctioning and the Threat of Regulation

When talking about the incident with me, Mariella presented herself and her team as the protectors of standards and compliance for the organization and the profession. She emphasized the need for transparency and independence between her department (the Awarding Body) and Geoff's department (a study center delivering corporate activity). She remarked:

> "When I was talking to Geoff about what the issues or concerns were that they struggled with, it was sort of drawing that scenario. The reality is ... we have everybody in one database. So therefore, Geoff's team is seeing the students that belong to competitors, i.e. study centres, and therefore they have privileged access to that information to be able to sell them something. And I guess when this

incident came up, whilst it was only one person that complained, and it was very interesting in terms of the logic when I was talking to Geoff; they seemed to be more concerned about the number of people that complained and therefore, dismissed it rather than really understanding the logic and the regulatory requirements we have legally ... As if to say well it was only one person, that doesn't really matter. So, what is the magic number when it becomes a problem? The reality, if you've breached something, even if you've done it once, you're in breach. Now, for those particular emails that went out, I could defend that because they were suspended members. Where I came into a challenging situation was the desire to send another email out, which I stopped going out, to all active students. And that's really when I had to put my foot down, which was challenging for Geoff because they perceive that I over-rode their authority and that I should have asked them first. The reality was they were not in the building. The email was about to go out. I had to make a snap decision to stop it so I could then find the time to sit and talk to Geoff, to help them understand why, potentially, that would be a real big problem. One of the things I'd said to him was I have to show that we're fair and transparent and actually what I did ... was print off our own code of conduct and highlighted our own code of conduct about how we should operate."

My conversations with Geoff painted a different picture of the data-sharing incident, presenting a scenario where they did in fact understand the potential conflict of interest, but had worked with Mariella's team ahead of the marketing campaign to find an acceptable solution:

> "This really goes back to a conversation that started late last year ... with [Mariella's team member], where we were getting towards the back of the e-learning development project and were starting to think about ways that we could leverage the asset and sell into more channels than just through the [department's] study centre, and to corporates. So, we believed that there was an opportunity for us to sell what I would call a study support aid, just like we sell our study guides. So, we knew that we wouldn't be able to market this standalone product as part of our study centre offering, so we didn't have any services around it, it was a pure study aid for [any] studying students. And we gained agreement from [Mariella's team member] that provided we used that kind of language, and that we did not attach any of the services that we make available to studying students through our study centre, that marketing the study aid to the [general] student population would be okay. So, we finished the development process over the winter and got into the position where we started to put our marketing plans together. Based on the conversation that

> we'd had with [Mariella's team member] we engaged with marketing and arranged to go to market, making very sure that this did not come across as an offer from the [association's] study centre. At the same time, we made the [external] study centres aware that they had access to this e-learning as well, at a discounted rate. So, we felt that we were creating a level playing field, selling directly to end users but also making the offer available through [other] study centres."

Notably, in the process of constructing their narratives both managers are doing "identity work," signaling the "kind of person I am" by elevating their "good" or "ethical" behavior. Mariella does this by describing how she "put her foot down" to protect the organization's reputation and interests, whereas Geoff voices the sentiment that he had "created a level playing field" through transparent and collaborative action with Mariella's team and the wider network of study centers. But there was ambiguity in Mariella's account. During the same conversation where she argued unequivocally that "a breach is a breach" of rules and regulations regardless of the scale, she also described having "wriggle room" on "bundling," whereby an individual is required to become an association member before obtaining a qualification, despite the regulators' distaste for it. She stated to me that the regulator has "gone as far as to say 'if you want to be an awarding body now you cannot bundle.' So, knowing that and knowing I've got a little bit of wriggle room, I'd certainly try and keep a low profile and what I wouldn't want (the regulator) to do is come in heavy on something else that actually we probably could have found a more creative way of dealing with ... and then they look into everything else." Such sentiments point to a tolerance for non-compliance as long as Mariella alone is the decision-maker of what kind and level of non-compliance is or is not deemed acceptable. What became clear is that the veracity, interpretation and application of the rules rests with Mariella, as "the only senior member who has a role that is both revenue generating and also has to protect public good and standards." Geoff described a feeling of "subservience" to his peer who has "ultimate control and authority about how regulations are applied."

The appropriation of the "protector of the public good" identity and the Awarding Body function has thus become institutionalized as a justified mechanism for policing and sanctioning other functions within the organization. Key to this surveillance activity is a) the co-optation of external experts to validate the director's technical knowledge, b) the threat of external regulation and mythologizing personal danger to the director, should non-compliance occur.

I became aware that Mariella had engaged personal contacts who had previously worked for the regulator to come into the association on two separate occasions; once to speak to Geoff in direct response to the above incident and once to deliver a more general briefing to staff ahead of a routine audit visit by the regulator. In relation to the specific incident, Geoff described having an hour with an ex-officer of the regulatory body to "talk through the scenario with him and understand what his perspective would have been if he'd been coming in and looking into the conflict of interest question." Geoff went on to position the regulatory expert's response as "non-committal" as "he said he needed to know much more about the scenario and the background before he could really give us any direct feedback." What the regulatory expert did re-enforce, however, was that the association "was in very safe hands from a regulatory point of view, provided Mariella is in charge." Geoff openly said that this not only reinforced the "subservient nature of our activity to Mariella's team" but that it also gave them "some comfort that the advice and direction we're getting from Mariella is not just their point of view … that it comes with, you know, practice and experience."

This sparked my interest because I had personally attended a recent workshop, commissioned by Mariella and delivered by an external regulatory expert who previously worked for the education regulator that was due to undertake a routine audit visit. The workshop was an open invitation and pitched as an opportunity "to hear more about the regulators," ahead of the visit. I had reflected in my fieldwork journal that the workshop appeared to be driven by four objectives. The first three – "to provide evidence of staff training to the regulators; to manage risk during the audit by providing key messages to staff on what/what not to say to the auditors; to educate staff in the risks of non-compliance with education regulations dictated by the regulator" – seem like pretty standard areas most organizations facing a regulatory audit would want to cover off ahead of an audit visit. It was the fourth that stood out. I noted that the workshop appeared to be designed "to promote Mariella's department as competent in their activity and provide reassurance that 'we were in safe hands.'" I revisited this in a conversation with the regulatory expert:

Carole: "In the workshop I experienced phraseology and messaging to inform those present about how competent Mariella's Department were at defending, protecting, doing good stuff on behalf of the rest of us. Was that intentional?"

Regulatory expert: "Nope. That must have been just because I believed it to be true. If I hadn't felt that, I wouldn't have let that impression come across, I don't think, but I think that was part of the attempt to be reassuring, that people haven't got to be terrified that [the regulator] would come in in a weeks' time and close the place down because there's a team of people who've got their finger on the pulse and they know what they're doing. I did deliberately try to get the message across that it's no small task to gain the confidence of [the regulator]."

Carole: "I also got a sense that you were trying to instruct us on what we should and should not say to the auditors, was that an objective?"

Regulatory expert: "Mariella focused in quite strongly on the fact that she was concerned that there would be people, who were relatively new, wouldn't have very much understanding about what [the regulator] was, let alone about what the implications of them coming to do a visit were. And so they felt that, to protect against any, you know 'foot in mouth' moments when [regulator] people turned up, this piece of work ought to be done. We both knew that [the regulator] have taken it upon themselves, not only to turn up anywhere unannounced if they choose to, although they rarely do it because they don't have the resource to do it, but also to decide to break out from the programme and just whizz off through corridors and into offices. We both knew that from the past and so we were both concerned that, whilst, if at all possible, the [regulatory] visitors would be contained and controlled in a room with chosen people, it was not impossible that they might ... one of them might just go off and, for example, look for blank certificates of the Awarding Body lying on tables and things so that anybody walking through could just take a handful and go away and then print on qualifications. So, we know that they've done that in the past. So that was another part of the anxiety."

Whether conscious or otherwise, the "in safe hands" narrative perpetuated by both regulatory experts depoliticizes Mariella's behavior while validating their technical knowledge. The terms adopted by the workshop facilitator – "anxiety," "concerned," "terrified," "protect" – are emotive and reinforce the threatening nature of regulation. In the first part of the extract given earlier, we see the regulatory expert remark that the reason people don't need to be terrified that the regulator will shut the association down is because of the competence of Mariella and her team.

There are also widespread myths of personal danger to Mariella, in the form of imprisonment, should a regulatory breach occur among lower–middle job grades in the association. I never uncovered the source of this story but had it recounted to me by five or six different colleagues during my fieldwork. As the opening of the chapter suggests, this myth has become a defining narrative that socializes and sanctions behaviors. Even at senior leadership team (Director) level, there is a strong sense of personal responsibility for the catastrophic consequences of non-compliance:

> "If I was to put our compliance at risk by creating a conflict of interest, a perceived conflict of interest, I could be responsible for [the association] not passing an audit or having corrective actions to do, which could threaten our future. If it was considered to be a serious breach and one that we failed to correct, we could have our awarding body status removed, which would mean our qualifications wouldn't sit on the framework, which would have some consequences in the market for the attractiveness of our qualification, particularly internationally. I understand the threats of not being compliant from a business point of view." (Geoff)

Geoff himself, as we saw earlier, perpetuates an equally powerful myth of personal consequences. Using serious humor, he creates a discourse among more junior staff that he is at personal risk of losing his job if he fails to meet the objectives of the "keeping me in a job project." In doing so, he elevates the importance and necessity of commercial behaviors and goals among a broader group.

This incident sheds some light on the structural sources and dynamics of power within the association. Within the now pervasive corporate logic, power and influence rest upon a particular function's contribution to revenue. There are principally four revenue streams that, from an economic perspective, constitute the association. As mentioned earlier, Mariella's team (the awarding body) is permitted to operate at "break even" due to the regulator's interest in and scrutiny of (price-based) accessibility to education. But, for the CEO and Geoff, this is in turn linked to the importance of being regulated within the international market, and therefore ultimately about protecting revenue generation. The CEO had explicitly stated his intention to reduce dependence on revenue from the awarding body and membership by increasing revenue from the corporate study center (i.e. delivery to corporate customers) and business development (i.e. sales of new products in new countries/sectors), as depicted in Figure 3.1.

In a climate where money is power, the directors responsible for the awarding body (Mariella) and membership were at risk of losing influence, whereas the directors of the corporate study center (Geoff) and business development stood to gain. By presenting the awarding body as the conscience of the association, Mariella attempts to position her team

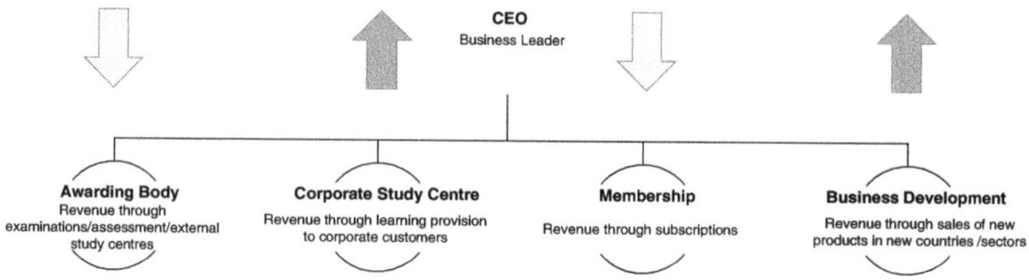

Figure 3.1 Power structures – association as four revenue channels.

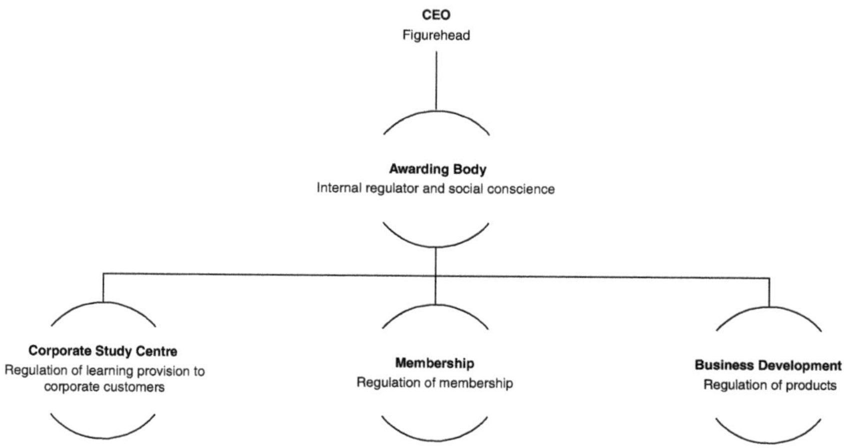

Figure 3.2 Power structures – association as awarding body.

as an "internal" regulator for social good, protecting the association from the legitimacy risks of being overly commercial. Such claims to a higher (moral) purpose for the awarding body could be understood as a tactic to circumvent Mariella's potential loss of (economically based) power, re-configuring social power structures as per Figure 3.2.

This chapter provides an appreciation of how two directors with conflicting agendas use discourse, politics and other influential actors to negotiate, persuade and peruse their own interests. Both protagonists draw on the CEO's agenda to reinforce their respective positions. Mariella, for example, brings the CEO's commitment to regulatory status into play through declaring that the CEO is "adamant that they want us to remain regulated" – albeit for reasons of market position. In addition and through the use of external experts, she presents herself and her team as competent to meet this important but difficult task. Conversely, Geoff arranged for a direct interface among him, Mariella and the CEO in order that the CEO "moderate" Mariella's "rigid application" of the regulations. Geoff describes using the CEO to mediate and move Mariella into a position where they provide a more practical and commercial application of risk than he was able to achieve independently. Arguably the regulatory compliance discourse has been developed as an important power resource or political tool in the types of "agonistic practices" we see here because of its utility in transcending individual (community and corporate) logics through more or less commercial applications of the rules for example.

The incident gained such notoriety within the association that it was commonly referred to as the "Mariella–Geoff Show," drawing some parallels to reality TV shows such as "Katie (Price) & Peter (Andre)" or "The Kardashians." Rather than "management" simply holding the power and discretion to define behaviors as acceptable or unacceptable and devise ways to manage (mis)behavior (Ackroyd & Thompson, 2003), managers themselves retreat into the kinds of misbehavior we see here. This undermines the (rational) principles of managerial work as we generally understand them. As a further illustration, a fellow director offered the following candid reflection on his views of the former and incumbent CEOs as managers:

> "They were both very insecure in their posts, this manifested itself in an absolute paranoia about keeping the trustees happy. I believe this was as a result of their previous baggage about being fired. It resulted in a reluctance to commit themselves to presenting original and innovative ideas in written words. In both cases this was, I think, a form of hiding their inability to make a firm decision which, if wrong, they might be blamed for. Whereas, if they swiped the genus of ideas from others' previous works, they could reference these as 'business as usual.'
>
> Both were not people orientated in the slightest; this on the face of it was more apparent with [the incumbent CEO] who seemed to treat all work colleagues, regardless of status, as chattels or in the extreme their feudal subjects. Both of them shared a belief that their opinions were the only ones that counted, although in [former CEO's] case he was more open to listening and subsequent persuasion than [incumbent CEO]. The admission of mistakes or the word sorry was almost exclusively absent as an aspect of their interaction with others. Another shared feature was an assumption that everyone who worked for them was by comparison mediocre and could not possibly be in their league.
>
> Enough of the parallels then, there were undoubtably some big differences in their respective styles. [The former CEO], if we looked at morality, always played with a 'Straight Bat,' having a strong

> moral compass that guided him to make decisions that were strictly within the regulatory and ethical framework. [The incumbent CEO] was always prepared to break the rules, after first ascertaining the probability of being found out. If their decision proved to be a bad one, they were particularly adept, I would almost say guileful, in covering up any problems or finding someone else to blame. [Incumbent CEO's] compass was one of 'true North' – at any cost.
>
> In relation to governance, [former CEO's] style was one of democracy and inclusiveness to achieve the ultimate purpose of the organization. In respect of [the association] these were the Charter objectives. [Incumbent CEO's] way was autocratic, guarded and exclusive to their own objectives and gain. They had scant regard for either Charter or not-for-profit objectives. A very contemporary personality comparison for them is that of Donald Trump. The component personality parts are all there: ego, narcissism, selfishness, superiority, arrogance, etc. Although [incumbent CEO] was not what I would regard as clever, they did have a certain 'Native Cunning' which they used to best effect in a manipulative and Machiavellian style with the trustees."

Managers, in shaping aspects of culture and social life within work organizations, suffer all the insecurities, inadequacies and need for purpose and meaning as everyone else (i.e. "the managed"), but perhaps with more catastrophic consequences to the organization and its inhabitants due to the formal authority they wield. The battle between the two central protagonists in this chapter is important insofar as it represents the bigger logic war within the association.

References

Ackroyd, S., & Thompson, P. (2003). *Organizational Misbehaviour*. London: Sage.

Bain, C. (2017). *Interplay of Intentions: An Ethnography of Institutional Work Within a Hybrid Organization*. Unpublished DBA (Doctoral) Thesis. Sheffield, UK: Sheffield Hallam University.

Bayma, T. (2012). Rational myth making and environment shaping: The transformation of the zoo. *The Sociological Quarterly*, *53*(1), 116–141.

Garfinkle, H. (1967). *Studies in Ethnomethodolgoy*. Englewood Cliff, New Jersey, USA: Prentice Hall.

Greenwood, R., & Hinings, C. R. (1993). Understanding strategic change: The contribution of archetypes. *Academy of Management Journal*, *36*, 1052–1081.

Meyer, J. W., & Rowan, B. (1977). Institutionalized organizations: Formal strcuture as myth and ceremony. *American Journal of Sociology*, *83*(2), 340–363.

Tolbert, P. S., & Zucker, L. G. (1996). The institutionalization of institutional theory. In S. Clegg, C. Hardy & W. Nord, *Handbook of Organization Studies* (pp. 175–190). London: Sage.
Zilber, T. (2002). Institutionalization as an interplay between actions, meanings and actors: The case of a rape crisis centre in Israel. *Academy of Management Journal*, *45*, 234–254.
Zilber, T. (2006). The work of the symbolic in institutional processes: Translations of rational myths in Israeli high tech. *Academy of Management Journal*, *49*(2), 281–303.

4 Symbols, Rhetoric and Strategizing

> It is salient that [the association] should focus its effort on membership retention as well as acquisition; it always costs less to service existing customers than it does to win new customers.
>
> (Membership Retention Strategy)

Serving the Members or the Institute? Commercialization and the Search for Growth

We saw that the hybrid nature of the association explicated in Chapter 2 means that decision-making and managerial action often occur in a contested field of tensions where managers appropriate the organizing principles and symbolic systems associated with their proffered logic, as explored in Chapter 3. Looking outwards, the general move towards a corporate logic fundamentally transformed the association's relationship with its members; repositioning them from a community of practice the association exists to serve to a resource to fund its global growth. I attended a senior leadership team meeting at which we were discussing the annual budget setting process. As a membership association, it was routine that annual membership fee setting was on the agenda, accompanied by a Membership Retention Strategy drafted by the director responsible for membership revenue. As the opening extract of this chapter shows, the strategy constitutes members as consumers of the association's products and accordingly advances an economic case for directing resources towards retention, based on cost efficiencies rather than development of the profession for wider public benefit.

Such a view of members sits uneasily with the ethos of the Charter, and the public presentation of the organization, which positions it as existing to serve its members:

> "[The association] was awarded the Charter in recognition of its leading role in supporting and furthering the interests of the [name removed] industry. We represent the interests of the profession and the views of our members. In fact, our special interest groups, online

> and face-to-face, encourage members to share their opinions and knowledge with the wider community. We're also directly involved in shaping [reference to professional function] policy for the UK Government and European Commission, and our consultative response process allows us to represent members' views at the highest level."
>
> (Association's Promotional Material)

Within the paper considered by the senior leadership team there was a proposal to increase U.K. membership fees by 2%. The paper stated that as 2% was the Bank of England's upper target for inflation in that financial year it would be hard to justify any more. In response, the CEO asked the directors for their views, arguing that in the previous year inflation had been lower and fees had been increased by 5% with no negative effect. In fact, he went on "membership was steaming ahead like a train" so why should we not increase it further as it seems to be "price inelastic." One of my peer group agreed, responding that we should charge, "as much as we think we can get away with as margin is high" whereas two argued for the minimum price increase as it was hard to justify anything more given that members were not receiving increased or enhanced benefits. Another peer argued against any membership fee increase, but posited that should this occur a percentage of the increase should be given to the association's subsidiary charity so that we "could use it for public good." After much debate, the decision was that a 5% increase would be recommended to the Board for their approval as "they (trustees) would change it anyway and as there was a lack of rigour in terms of indices to base our decision, 5% was as good a number as 2%."

Three things were striking in this conversation. First, no one challenged the presentation of members as consumers. During my early years at the association, members were seen to be part of the wider community of practice the organization exists to develop and therefore membership fee revenue would be used to develop the profession in a broad sense rather than simply servicing members as direct consumers. Positioning members in a transactional relationship with the organization originates from a corporate logic and undertakes that in return for their fee, members (as consumers) expect a personal tangible benefit such as free or discounted access to resources and events. An alternative perspective would be that members consider themselves to be part of a community of practice (Lave & Wenger, 1991; Hoadley, 2012), share a passion for the profession and assume some responsibility for its continual development. Within this orientation, it is possible that members consider their fees to be a donation to support the development of their community of practice – a personal investment for collective benefit. Second, by making a proposal to transfer a proportion of the increased fee to the subsidiary charity, that colleague constitutes public good activity as a sub-set of the main organization rather than representative of its core purpose; an approach akin to corporate social responsibility or corporate philanthropy. Although this particular colleague presents themself as the "protector of public good" (see Chapter 3), they are – perhaps unconsciously – nevertheless reproducing a member as consumer perspective and thus a (albeit softer) corporate logic within the association. Third, outside the conversation around the subsidiary charity, no one asked how the additional revenue from membership fees would be used. The generation of more money was taken as the objective in and of itself.

Within the increasingly corporate organizing logic of the association, being "global" in terms of footprint, membership and brand awareness, was paramount (see Chapter 2). Returning to the role description for Mariella – positioned as the only director with a revenue generating *and* public good mandate – in Chapter 3, there is a fixation on globalization through:

- being the global standard setter for the profession (A1/A2/A12);
- meeting global market needs (A3/A4);
- developing and managing global education products (A4);
- ensuring world class status of educational programmes (A5);
- leading representation in the global education arena and corporate market to support reputational and business growth (A10);
- maintaining and growing a global network of education providers (A11).

By the time fieldwork commenced, the global focus was most commonly geared towards serving a growthist agenda. This stood in stark contrast to my early years at the association where the discursive justification of global presence primarily rested upon representation of the profession (and members) within a given country context, with little concern for revenue generation beyond achieving a break-even position:

> "During the [previous 3-year] plan the balance of UK vs. International activity was roughly 75:25. This represented a shift from the previous plan and included the setting up of [overseas office], the launch of our qualifications in China, increased support for members in Africa, expansion in the Gulf States and a higher level of engagement with global corporates. In addition to these five areas of activity, which we will continue to support and develop in the new plan, we have agreed to increase our influence in Europe through more lobbying/representation, knowledge development and engagement with corporates, both direct and via appropriate alliances."
>
> (3-year Strategic Plan written by former CEO)

The CEO at the time applied his familiar mantra: "If we do the right thing, the money will follow." In some ways this was borne out when, rather ironically, one of the major international offices began to make significant financial losses following the explicit shift in purpose from service to members and the wider profession, to revenue generation. A colleague with almost 20 years' service within the association commented:

> "... Demonstrating that we reinvest what we earn to deliver our charter objectives more effectively is hard to do and ... people tend to fall back on this [accepted strapline that we make money to do more 'good stuff'] as a way of legitimising expansion plans without thinking through what this means. For example, for me there is a dichotomy between what we say the purpose of international expansion is and with what we task it with delivering. We set up the outposts to be commercial, they are not set up or positioned as not for profits, they are commercial companies which are to all intents and purposes sales offices where even membership is a product with a price tag. We measure their success on revenue and net profit. They are treated as net contributors to [association] coffers (and if they don't contribute cash they are judged to be failures). Yet we say, without any sense at all that this is disingenuous, that they are some sort of outpost for standards, carrying the [association's] banner for the greater good. For me, this is the fundamental problem for our international offices, we set them up, staff them and evaluate them as commercial enterprises but somehow expect them to fulfil the public benefit agenda and deliver the mission."

I recollect a stark example of this from my own day-to-day work. The CEO had previous experience working in China and Hong Kong and, as we had an established educational programme in China, they decided that China would be a target for growth. Rather than the association continuing to accredit Chinese universities to deliver its syllabus, the CEO wanted to open an international office in China.

The financial conditions for opening a "business" in China, however, are complex and quite unique. To register a Wholly Foreign-Owned Enterprise (WFOE) (i.e. a trading organization providing services), the association would be required to deposit approximately £100,000–£120,000 in a Chinese bank account. This cash investment would need to remain in the Chinese bank account, and is often hard to extract once deposited. The WFOE would be required to trade in Renminbi, a currency that isn't fully convertible, or Hong Kong Dollars. The entity would be required to have premises within China and to employ only Chinese staff, or all revenue made within China would be subject to a 10% withholding tax.

Unwilling to make such an investment, the CEO attempted to circumvent this requirement by setting up a "representational office" limited to market research and brand development. Such entities are not permitted to make any profit in China. The CEO's intention was to exploit this loophole by utilizing the representational office to develop brand awareness and build networks in China, then direct any subsequent profit-making activity through the association's corporate trading subsidiary in the U.K. The chartered status of the association, and its "representational" mandate, was in effect used as a Trojan Horse to enable "free" access to the Chinese market for revenue generating purposes. Ultimately, this approach failed, and the office closed as the association's legal advisors in China continually discouraged this practice and Chinese corporations themselves were reluctant to flout in-country regulations.

What's in a Name?

The overt strategy to align all activities to the purpose of global organizational growth was accompanied by changes in "every day talk" that paid homage to the military origins of strategy (Bracker, 1980). There was a discursive shift towards the corporate world where "the institute" became "the business," and conversations injected a previously alien language of "segmented customized offerings," "profit maximization," "market penetration," "market share," "making the organization unassailable" and "building a war chest for potential acquisitions."

The balanced score card depicted in Figure 4.1 provides an apt illustration of how every element – operational, people, membership/community – was reduced to a financial Key Performance Indicator. Servicing the growth of the association through its "customer base" had become the end game. As one colleague put it:

> "[The] metrics are all about money and absolute numbers. We do not include softer measures based on the charter objects. When setting strategy, the Trustees and its predecessors have asked us time after time to have a public good theme and to measure how well we are doing on these softer issues. We don't do that because it is just too difficult to measure things that can't be easily quantified and commentaries are largely meaningless if scrutinised. But as long as measurement, success and reward is based on commercial metrics the essential dichotomy at the heart of [the association] in its current form is irreconcilable."

Table 4.1 below maps out the strategy of the association at one point during the former and incumbent CEOs' terms of office, comparing the stated purpose or goal of the organization and the priority strategic themes.

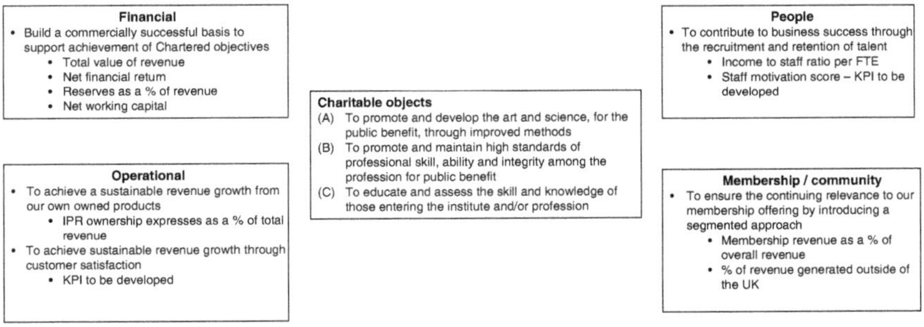

Figure 4.1 Balanced score card from 3-year strategy.

At face value, the strategic themes show much overlap, focusing on brand, membership, knowledge and standards, but their purpose differs. We see the former CEO return to the Charter multiple times (rows 2 and 3) and constitute knowledge development as the cornerstone of the association's work, both for educating members of the profession and influencing/advocating on its behalf (rows 2, 3 and 4). In contrast, the incumbent CEO positions knowledge as serving the association's reputation as the "go-to" place or first reference point and as a means to generate sales income (row 2). The sole mention of the Charter (row 1) is linked to brand value and underwriting the philanthropy undertaken by the subsidiary charity. The prevalent thread is growth (rows 2, 3 and 4) and the CEO introduced the strategic themes with the statement:

> "Driving the [association] to £50m in five years requires changing our mind-set and how we operate from SME to that of a mid-sized operation. It will be important to continue a balanced corporate and global growth in all three areas of Corporate Services, Professional Development and Membership, which will require 'Sustainable Thinking.' To achieve this requires utilisation of our stakeholder community."
>
> (Incumbent CEO, 3-year Strategic Plan)

Notably, the CEO positions the association as a Small-to-Medium Enterprise (SME) – a term commonly used to describe corporate entities rather than charities or social purpose organizations. In fact, the association would be considered very large against a charity referent group (a "major" charity by the National Council for Voluntary Organisation's definition). The idea of "utilizing" stakeholders (in this case members) to achieve growth is again akin to corporate organization behaviour. On introducing their priority strategic themes, the former CEO also talks of securing the association's success and of sustainability,

Table 4.1 Comparison of strategy within community and corporate organizing logics

Strategy within the community logic (Former CEO)	*Strategy within the corporate logic (Incumbent CEO)*
Organizational goal	
Our ultimate purpose is to deliver public benefit with organizations being the main "instrument" to achieve this by helping them to make and spend money in an appropriate, responsible way through excellent [function] management. Our Charter mandates us to meet four strategic imperatives: to promote and represent the profession; to help organizations; to help individuals and; to develop an appropriate body of knowledge.	• The profession's global standard • The first port of call for all [function-related] knowledge • The largest and financially strongest of professional institutes
Strategic themes and theme goals	
1 Brand	1 Public good
a The [association's] brand and reputation are crucial to the institute's success. It is essential that the brand appeals to and is seen as relevant to a wide range of audiences. Brand recognition is currently better among some audiences than others and the plan for [the next three years] will be to continue to strengthen the brand generally and, in key markets we identify, reinforce with appropriate sub-brands.	a To be a recognized leader for promotion and delivery of public good and enhance the public's perception of the profession and the institute as its global champion. To achieve this goal we must maintain a powerful brand value that is firmly rooted in our Charter and Charity status. This represents the continuing core purpose to develop and champion the sustainable, beneficial impact of professional [function] on society, both nationally and internationally. It will underwrite the philanthropic aims and actions of the [subsidiary charity].
2 Key audiences, customers and clients	2 Membership transformation – Customized solutions
a Our Charter requires [the association] to help	a To ensure the continuing relevance of our offering, by

Strategy within the community logic (Former CEO)	*Strategy within the corporate logic (Incumbent CEO)*
individuals to develop themselves and organizations to improve their [function] performance and we do this by providing products and services that are relevant to their needs and up to date both in content and delivery method. b We are also mandated to represent the discipline and the people working in it to a wide range of audiences and we do this through a combination of "quiet" influencing and "noisy" PR.	introducing a segmented communities approach in order to maintain/grow our global community and expand our influence
3 Knowledge development a Knowledge development is a key Charter objective. We need to see the activity as constantly filling a reservoir that feeds all of our "products," from course books, qualifications, training programmes, to "flat" knowledge delivered via the Website, certification, conferences, publications and responses to government consultation papers.	3 Knowledge – "[Association] First" a To be recognized as the primary reference point for [function-related] knowledge, acting as a knowledge hub for the profession b To deliver sustainable sales of products and services with [the association] to be seen as the "go-to" place to help develop organizational know-how.
4 Priority subjects a In addition to continuing to work on all aspects of [function] management, there are some issues that we believe are so important that we must give them	4 Global reach – hub and satellite model a To have a presence in all the main commercial "hubs" across the globe. Continuing global growth is fundamental to our growth agenda in

(*Continued*)

Table 4.1 (Continued)

Strategy within the community logic (Former CEO)	*Strategy within the corporate logic (Incumbent CEO)*
special attention and deal with them in a high-profile way. Three priority subjects have been identified to date (with the proviso that one or more may reduce in importance over the course of the plan and other topics may emerge): • Globalization (develop White Paper and representation) • CSR/sustainability (review and update of current knowledge) • The future of [function] management (visioning and academic research, etc).	supporting the most global of professions.
5 Standards b [The association] sets standards for individuals (ethical, qualification and membership at a range of levels) and organizations (Certification, at two levels). These standards are closely linked to brand, which they enhance. [The association's] standards are becoming increasingly recognized worldwide as relevant, objective and impartial and this recognition is a key USP for the institute with all our audiences.	5 Global standard "[Association] inside" and license to practice. a To be recognized as the home of the global standards for [the professional function] and the authority for the Licence to Practice, which is acknowledged as the world-class benchmark for professionals. b To provide an education offering that will bring young people into the profession and take them on a life-long journey to become truly global strategic leaders.

but in relation to achieving sustainable public benefit rather than corporate and global growth for no other reason than the growth itself:

> "The challenge we face in designing our corporate plan is to ensure that [the association] operates successfully and prospers but does it in such a way that it also achieves (and can continue to achieve in a sustainable way) its public benefit objectives."
>
> (Former CEO, 3-year Strategic Plan)

The adoption of code names such as "Project Emerald," "Project Liberty" and "Project Eagle" also became commonplace during the incumbent CEO's term of office. Each of these strategic initiatives involved a degree of secrecy, or in military strategy terms "deceiving the enemy." Project Emerald involved the removal of the Managing Director (MD) of an international office due to a failure to serve the association's interests; the role incumbent was depicted as a "maverick" that was not hitting revenue targets. One aspect of this project was the relocation of a previously U.K.-based director who was leading a Middle East initiative at the time prior to the MD's sacking in order to facilitate a transition period. Project Liberty and Project Eagle related to anti-slavery and risk reduction campaigns. Both campaigns involved development of associated chargeable products targeted at the corporate market and were developed in secrecy in order to establish a position of dominance within that market.

Organizational strategy, within the now prevalent commercial framing of the association explicated in Chapter 2, thus placed the association on a war footing, depicting competition as more and more fierce and survival increasingly problematic:

> "In common with many professional organisations, we will face significant challenges over the next Strategic Plan period. The continuing effect of the global economic downturn and the tightening on personal finances is especially impacting on our membership proposition ... As part of our strategic planning we recognise that as we grow so may our competitors. To ensure that we remain agile and retain and develop our market position there will be an increased focus on competition with on-going competitor analysis to help us to determine how we should differentiate ourselves through our brand, products and services."
>
> (3-Year Strategic Plan)

The solution, rather than service and cooperation, was about exposing opponents' or competitors' weaknesses; concentrating resources to attack an opponent's weakness; overwhelming selected markets or market segments; establishing a leadership position of dominance in certain markets;

then expanding from the base created to dominate a broader area. This was captured in the strap line of the so-called corporate strategy "[Name of association] First." The phrase "[Association] First" was first used by a board member and in relation to knowledge resources in a Board Strategy meeting. The board member said "who cares where people go next [to find what they are looking for], as long as they came to [the association] first, to understand best practice." The board member was arguing that it did not matter where or from whom a member of the profession eventually received support, so long as the association was leading "the art and science" by signposting and brokering access to high-quality knowledge sources and support services (i.e. "how to"/good practice guides, codes of practice, etc.). In a political nod to the Board, the CEO adopted this phrase as the strategy's strapline but appropriated its meaning as an expression that the association must "come first" in terms of market position.

When we (the senior leadership team) considered "new" activity during the former CEO's term of office, they would always say "we need to be the second mouse to the cheese." This evoked imagery of the first mouse going into the trap and taking all the risk and consequences of the trap activating, with the second mouse being able to approach the cheese with an understanding of how the trap worked, thus reducing risk and increasing the chance of success. That is not to say that the former CEO was risk averse – that was not my experience – but they were always mindful of the role and status of the association and that its funds were "public money." As such, any expenditure and associated risk must be carefully considered.

Strategy under the current CEO had become analogous with the art of war. Indeed, in a synthesis of Chinese general Sun Tzu's classic work on military strategy, *The Art of War*, from over two millennia ago McNeilly (1996) shows how Tzu's strategic principles can be applied to twenty-first century business in *The Art of Business*. The text covers many of the aforementioned aspects of strategy and associated tactics in which the association now engaged. I sense that the incumbent CEO would have enjoyed this comparison, as they often talked about their history degree and their interest in military history; perhaps their approach to "business" really was grounded in military history books.

Good to Great

Accompanying this sense of competitiveness was a growing preoccupation with internal and external awards symbolizing the status of both the association and the individuals within it. Internally, staff members were rated against three categories: under performer, good performer or great performer. To be rated great, staff members needed to not only show consistent performance against the Personal Qualities and Behaviour

Framework for their level, but also exceed their agreed objectives and achieve goals beyond their own role. Those receiving a great rating received financial and non-financial rewards, such as the commission of a caricature portrait of the individual, which hung in the association's boardroom.

I was interested in what the association was recognizing as "great" performance and therefore read the testimonials of individuals who achieved this rating. Over a 3-year period, a total of 17 awards were made. Table 4.2 provides illustrative extracts of the testimonials and highlights the dominance of and value placed upon commerciality in what is deemed "great." Of the 17 awards, only one connected to Charter objects relating to developing the profession and achieving public good (see final row titled "Campaigns"). This citation related to an anti-slavery campaign, which could be framed as public good, but as discussed earlier was also about being first to market.

External accolades coveted by the CEO included The Louis Armstrong CEO Leadership Award from memcom and the *Sunday Times* 100 Best (Nonprofit) Companies to Work For. With regard to the former, I remember at the end of a routine 1:1 with the CEO (my line manager), them saying "I'd really like to win a best CEO award ... can I leave that with you?"' I was then chased by the marketing team for a nomination statement but fudged some kind of response and was relieved the following year when the association sponsored the award so could not make a nomination.

The Best Companies journey has a number of interesting aspects to it. As an institute, we had historically used an established culture survey to try and understand "how it feels to work around here." A decision was taken at a senior leadership team meeting to pursue the 100 best companies award, which requires participation in the best companies accreditation (star rating) system, judged via results of a compulsory survey. Organizations then pay an extra fee if they wish to be entered for the "Top 100," as it was termed by the CEO. Notably, the team responsible for organizational development referred to it as Best Companies accreditation and were interested in the survey results as a barometer for staff engagement and experience. The CEO was interested in the Top 100 award and never outwardly acknowledged the category in which the association was entered "100 Best Not-for-Profits". It seemed to me that at the point we switched from the customary culture survey, it ceased to be about "how it feels to work around here" and became about the prize of "Top 100." There were subsequent incidents of certain directors berating their team if the "scores" from their department let the association down, or rather put its Top 100 ranking in jeopardy. Within formal internal documentation, the explicit rationale

Table 4.2 "Great" citations

Revenue growth	"[xxx] had a fantastic year, delivering above and beyond what is expected in their role. Our achievements include: • smashing their sales target and bringing in an additional 80% of revenue • selling three [product name removed] • using [system name removed] effectively to record opportunities and build good relationships with the wider sales community • supporting the team with a successful telesales campaign to support the launch of the [product name removed]."
Profit growth	"[xxx] has excelled in all areas of their role and surpassed all targets and objectives set ... Their dedication is un-questionable and their contribution is well recognized. It is however, their contribution to cost savings and efficiencies for cost reduction and scalable delivery that has directly contributed to the outstanding achievement of achieving positive NFR for the first time. S's efforts this year have seen them achieve savings well in excess of 200k which exemplifies their deep knowledge of delivery costs along with the innovation and dedication to 'make it happen.'"
Supporting globalization	"[xxx] was rated Great this year for her work on the finance project which was the Group Finance Team's biggest adventure in the last 20 years I believe, and excelled at taking the challenge of integration and implementation forward through to a successful Phase 1 Go-Live ... At times, [xxx] has needed to be strong in her approach to ensure controls are adhered so that we continue to maintain financial stability and transparency globally, which I believe continues to work in our favour."
Reducing dependency on suppliers[1]	"[xxx] led the project to launch a new facility for students which now delivers a high-quality high-end product where students can self-serve a significant amount of support which has reduced the amount of work on support staff. W's creativity has ensured the development of new and better content, in order to move away from suppliers and increase own our own IP." "Development of our owned IP and taking direct responsibility for tutor resourcing and programme quality assurance are game changers for [the association]. In pursuit of these objectives [xxx] has applied their considerable knowledge, skills

	and experience to create a student centred delivery capability where cost, quality and agility are driving significantly improved levels of performance and will contribute towards eliminating £1.35 million of losses from the P&L in FY15."
Developing brand	"This year, [xxx's] day job expanded to include Events and leading the embedding of a global PR strategy which delivered the highest AVE (Advertising Value Equivalent) we have ever seen, at £33 million. But on top of all that [xxx] has managed and delivered a complex tender, which has resulted in the move to [supplier name removed]. It's pretty difficult to move away from a supplier that has been in place for 18 years, and with whom you have built up a strong relationship, but [xxx] was unflinching in their commitment to using this opportunity to make a step change for [the association]."
Campaigns	"This year [xxx] has led on two key projects with great results. Project Liberty is the work that we have done with the [name of external organization removed] on the anti-slavery agenda. To support that, [xxx] led on the delivery of the Ethics test, which many of you here have undertaken. Project Eagle is a strategic initiative with [name of consultancy house removed] on providing the [product name removed] to our corporate contacts."

Source: Adapted from Bain (2017).

for "Good to Great" and "Top 100" was about on-going global success, PR and the kudos of being an elite organization:

> "Also fundamental to our on-going success is the development of our staff on the 'Good to Great' journey. Pay for performance is embedded, and [the institute's] Talent and Business Leaders Group are being encouraged to take ownership. Delivering to our global agenda, our staff expansion strategy will be to prioritize appointments from developing internal staff, with the exception of highly "technical" needs from the open market. Our strategy will also be to use an active graduate and apprentice scheme as the prime driver to enhance our staff base both in the U.K. and globally, so ensuring we build for the future. Our IIP Silver Award will be targeted to reach Gold level and we will endeavour to achieve the '*Sunday Times* Top 100' Institution for employee satisfaction."
>
> (3-Year Strategy)

> "Following the shift in [the association's] culture score to one that 'enables growth and high performance' and [our] attainment of the Investors in People Silver Award, 'Top 100' has been identified as [the association's] next target accreditation … If [the association] is successful, potential business benefits include:
>
> - High-profile media attention through publication of the lists;
> - Published on "Best Companies Guide" Website and job board with best companies index score and star rating;
> - Publicity from the lists have proved to help attract talented people and retain the best employees;
> - Kudos associated with being one of the very few, elite organizations carrying the accreditation logo (logo and star rating can be used in marketing and recruitment activity);
> - Year on year results allow identification of trends and improvements within [the association]; and
> - Benchmarking with the best – performance results from the survey can be directly compared with other organizations that make the lists." (Internal Paper/Business Case)

As introduced in Chapter 2 and illustrated throughout this chapter, the new strategy and associated articulation of mission and vision represented a key mechanism for the incumbent CEO to re-write the organizational script. Scripts offer an image of the organization as a whole, producing conceptions of structure and responsibility in ways that specify activities, outcomes, what knowledge is valued, roles, duties and authority (Kuhn, 2008). They represent, mediate, point attention towards, discipline and connect people and practices; they are a reference point, encouraging inhabitants of organizations to prioritize the collective good, as defined by the script. Once scripts become reified (treated as objects) their socially constructed nature is overlooked, concealing the ideological foundations on which they rest, nevertheless creating the rules of the game to which inhabitants orientate (Smith, 2004) and assign identity, motive and obligation (Cooren, 2004). Because scripts define boundaries and exert "official" influence or authority over practices, they are sites of struggle over meaning among those parties with a vested interest in advancing their particular framing of organizational purpose. We saw this ideological war play out within the managerial ranks in Chapter 3.

In Part II, we provide an account of the managerial work and organizational processes involved in transforming the trajectory of the organization and its manifestations in different aspects of organizing including organizational structure, recruitment and reward, governance and leadership. We suggest that it is this institutional work that enables organizational inhabitants to "connect personal identities and biographical narratives to the firm and its operations" (Kuhn, 2008, p. 1239) and thus consent, albeit precariously, to the new script.

Note

1 The association has a legacy of working with suppliers owned intellectual property (IP) (products). Where there is a reference to creating focal organization owned IP this refers to creating products that are owned by the association and not the supplier.

References

Bain, C. (2017). *Interplay of Intentions: An Ethnography of Institutional Work Within a Hybrid Organization.* Unpublished DBA (Doctoral) Thesis. Sheffield, UK: Sheffield Hallam University.

Bracker, J. (1980). The historical development of the strategic management concept. *Academy of Management Review*, *5*(2), 219–224.

Cooren, F. (2004). Textual agency: How texts do things in organizational settings. *Organization*, *11*, 373–393.

Hoadley, C. M. (2012). What is a community of practice and how can we support it? In G. H. Jonassen, & S. M. Land, *Theoretical Foundations of Learning Environments* (2nd Ed., pp. 287–300). New York, NY: Routledge.

Kuhn, T. (2008). A communicative theory of the firm: Developing an alternative perspective on intra-organizational power and stakeholder relationships. *Organization Studies*, *29*, 1227–1254.

Lave, J., & Wenger, E. (1991). *Situated Learning: Legitimate Peripheral Participation.* Cambridge: Cambridge University Press.

McNeilly, M. (1996). *Sun Tzu and the Art of Business: Six Strategic Principles for Managers.* New York: Oxford University Press.

Smith, J. D. (2004). A précis of a communicative theory of the firm. *Business Ethics: A European Review*, *13*, 317–331.

Part II

Transforming Organizational Trajectory

Part II provides an account of the managerial work and organizational processes involved in transforming the organization's raison d'être and its manifestations in organizational structure, recruitment and reward, governance and leadership.

5 Structuring for Purpose

> "We need to be more professional, big business-like, and have money-making activity to meet the significant challenges with the continuing effect of global economic downturn."
>
> (CEO, 3-Year Strategy)

Corporate Philanthropy: Charity as Something we "do," not What we "are"

As we have shown, the former CEO's framing of the association was simple, had clarity of purpose, and was aligned with organizational "type." In essence: "We are a chartered body and we exist to do public good. We do public good by delivering the four Charter objectives ... money is our oxygen, but making money is not the end game." The association's structure reflected the same characteristics (see Figure 5.1).

In this structure, all areas had a focus on delivering to the Charter; international offices were positioned under membership and measured on developing the number of members and students in the region and providing local membership services. The organization's legal status as a Charity was integral to Charter objectives, both focusing on public benefit.

There was a single subsidiary Limited Company set-up to manage the provision of one service that was delivered solely to the profession, but which did not contribute directly to Charter objectives. It was therefore treated as a distinct commercial entity that delivered significant funds to the association.

Under the incumbent CEO, various aspects of the organization were restructured in pursuit of commercialization, growth and globalization, becoming increasingly complex as the CEO tried to negotiate the various demands, regulations and legitimacy judgements of different stakeholder groups in the U.K. and internationally (see Figure 5.2).

The development of complex and at times contradictory structures accompanied the growth of the association, not least through the creation and maintenance of unnecessary charitable and non-charitable subsidiaries. For example, each international office was set up as a

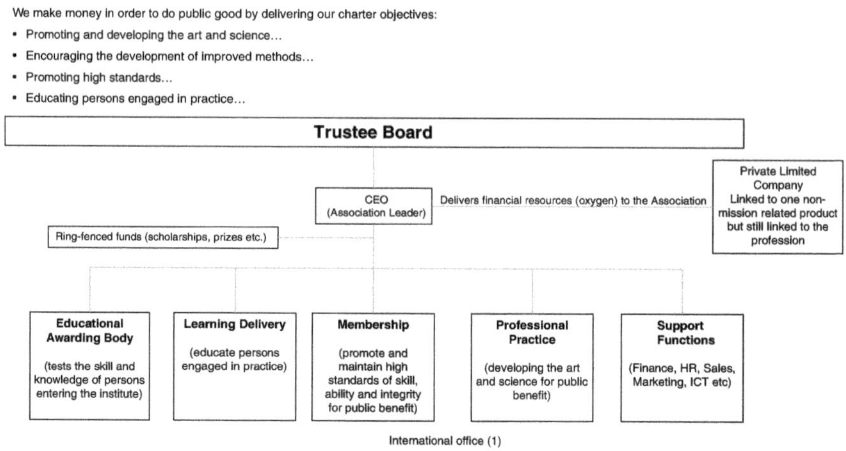

Figure 5.1 Organizational structure – former CEO.

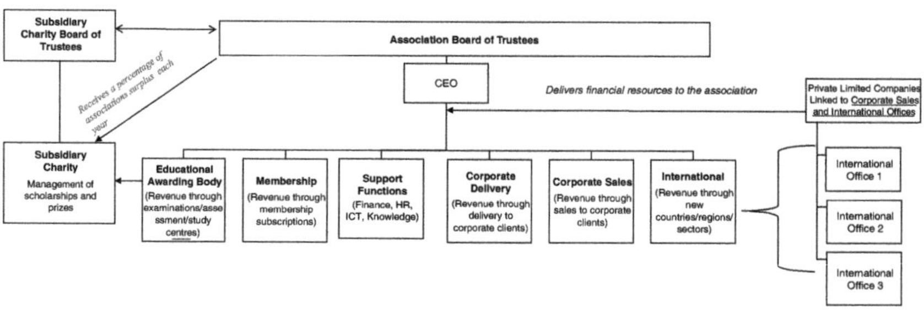

Figure 5.2 Organizational structure – incumbent CEO.

wholly owned limited company in its own right, requiring governance, HR, finance and other infrastructure. The activities of the existing trading subsidiary ceased, but the entity was (unnecessarily) maintained as a contracting vessel for the association's delivery of in-company training programmes to corporate clients within the U.K. Interestingly, corporate delivery in the U.K. would fall within the Charter and charitable objectives. Under English Charity Law this would be classed as mission-related trading income and could therefore legitimately be undertaken by the association within its day-to-day work. We saw in Chapter 3 how managers can, for example, artfully exploit such structural ambiguities to create perceptions of conflicts of interest and marginalize corporate delivery as "lesser" in moral and social good terms.

As shown in Figure 5.2, the association had, for a long time, benefitted from a ring-fenced fund to provide financial awards to students – e.g. for "best marks." Despite their long-term role within the association, these funds were allocated to a new subsidiary, set up as a linked charity with its own board of trustees, separate financial systems and branding from the parent charity. The association also made a commitment to making an annual donation to the subsidiary based on the financial surplus of the association. As illustrated in Chapter 2, a common narrative within the association was that the subsidiary charity was "a small part" or "side arm" and that it had been "divorced from the main business" so it could be "properly managed" and not "generally get lost in the mainstream business." Though there was no technical or legal necessity to decouple the charitable activity of the subsidiary from the parent charity, symbolically it served as a powerful message that the "core" organization did not need to be overly concerned with social impact in "everyday business" as this was achieved through the charitable subsidiary. Such a model is closely aligned to private sector models of corporate social responsibility or corporate philanthropy. At the same time, the existence of both the charitable and trading company subsidiaries could be mobilized to defend the main charity from any internal and/or external criticism of being "too commercial." The colleague who at one time was responsible for drafting the association's annual return to the U.K. charity regulator, the Charity Commission, recounted the challenges she encountered in trying to meet the increasingly tough "public benefit" test:

> "I went to a conference on it [the public benefit requirement]. And I sat there thinking 'oh, God, we don't meet any of these criteria.' I came back thinking we've got to really, really up what we say we do in the public benefit arena. And I happened to be thinking about the restricted fund and I thought hang on, we don't do anything that's philanthropic because as part of this presentation, they were talking about philanthropic arms of commercial companies, a lot of big companies that would have a philanthropic foundation or something as a way of trying to, you know, tick the CSR box or improve their brand or whatever. And so this word philanthropy kept coming up. And I thought well, there's nothing at all that we do that's philanthropic. And I'd been talking to a contact at [name of organization] and they have an entire philanthropic arm which actually gives money to company secretaries who fall on hard times. I mean, they sort of have ... [a] benevolent fund, they have ... visitors who go around and look after elderly chartered secretaries ... so they have this really big thing that they do. And then I started looking into others and these people have got a charity that does this and we have ... we don't do anything charitable."
>
> **Carole:** "Despite being a charity?"
>
> "Despite being a charity, we don't do anything charitable. And so I started talking to people and thinking about it. And I can't remember who it was I spoke to originally, but it ended up being a paper ... I put

> to the board saying 'we've got this fund, guys, do you think it would be a good idea to actually do something more philanthropic with it and find a way of building up the reserves in it so that we can do more stuff' … But the original cause came from the new requirements …
>
> It was happening at the time that charities were beginning to be discredited, so there was a lot of talk about the amount of cash charities spent on running themselves … you know, by the time they've paid their bonuses and everything there was nothing left to give to the poor. So there's a lot of criticism of that and a lot of criticism of chuggers and things like that … do you know where the money you're putting in that tin is going? Is it going to buy the chief executive a new Jag? That kind of thing was coming out so a lot of charities were struggling and seeing drops in … donations because the public were getting very cynical … so society was getting cynical, the public benefit test came in."
>
> **Carole:** "I'm simplifying what I think I heard you say. When you went to that [event], you went, 'huh … we won't necessarily be able to fulfil that public benefit test … what are other similar organisations similar to us doing … and then those other similar organisations are actually mimicking commercial organisations?"
>
> "Yes. Yes. Yes. Yes."

Such "Greenwashing" – spending more time, effort and money on looking like or claiming to be socially responsible than actually implementing responsible practices – among corporate entities has received much public and scholarly attention over recent years (Laufer, 2003; Alves, 2009; Nyilasy et al., 2014). Yet this type of "decoupling" is, perhaps erroneously, assumed to be absent from the charity world. There is a danger that this phenomenon of intentionally "faking it" becomes increasingly prevalent with the commercialization and managerialization of nonprofits, or where information asymmetries between stakeholders such as those discussed in this chapter are created (Crilly et al., 2012).

On engaging with some of the early findings from my fieldwork, a colleague captured the hybridity identity "war" (Kerr, 1963) taking place within the association as follows:

> "The comments about the charitable subsidiary are revealing and ring true. For me, they confirm that for some people the subsidiary has become a handy repository for all the charitable values. By hiving off the charity aspect to somewhere clearly identifiable as being for the public good, it is almost as though some people feel this box is now ticked and the rest of the organization can now be more overtly commercial. Before we had the charitable subsidiary the mix of charitable and commercial was more complex and subtle because

> it wasn't possible to draw absolute lines between public benefit and business activities. There is a risk that people will over-rationalise in a desire to simplify things and decide that everything that isn't the charity subsidiary is, by exception, commercial. I fully recognise that the subsidiary is for some a symbolic and low priority activity which ticks the charity box, freeing them to concentrate on making money.
>
> Structurally, the limited companies are subordinate to the main body so it would be legitimate to view them as engines to deliver fuel to the parent. But then, the [subsidiary charity] is also subordinate to the main body, and the main body itself engages directly in commercial activity. No wonder people struggle to pin down what kind of organisation they are working for."

Another reading is that the charitable and charter status of the association were now actively appropriated to gain competitive advantage in various ways. First, the idea was presented that the only benefit to being a charity (as far as the CEO was concerned) was "tax exemption." Second, its legal status, organizational form and regulated activities differentiated the association from "charlatans" and other "cheque-book [i.e. money-orientated] institutions." The senior manager who presented themself as the protector of public good within the association in Chapter 3, remarked:

> "[The length of] Our presence here [in the U.K.], our reputation, and the UK being a mature market, would accept on face value and wouldn't give two hoots about it [the association being a regulated education Charity]. The bizarre thing that's driven all this actually is our international expansion and the fact international markets need to be satisfied that we're not a charlatan. Because there are so many different institutions. And therefore how can international markets distinguish legitimate institutions that have a public good mandate and that were there to make money to do things and not do things to make money, as opposed to what I would call a cheque book institute, which is there for one thing ... behind this façade of the word institute, there's a limited company with people wanting to make profit."

Ironically, our own institute could be accused of creating exactly this façade, given the nature of its current strategy (refer to Chapter 4), and the apparent use of charitable status as a ***Trojan Horse*** (Pache & Santos, 2013) to "beat the competition." This creates something of a paradox in that although elite actors aligned to the corporate logic use structure to sideline and reduce the level of influence and presence of "charity" [through the subsidiary], they simultaneously recognize its value to differentiate the organization in commercial conversations. This suggests that it is something that is valued for its moral legitimacy to specific audiences, but for the purposes of competitive advantage.

Governance: Bring me "Big Business People"

The evolution of organizational structure was accompanied by governance-level alterations. This involved the reformation of a large board of 47 trustees into a representational group of 62 members. Though this group lost their trustee status they were positioned as "the Institute's representative and advisory body, elected from the global membership … the 'conscience' of the Institute … [which] holds the Board of Trustees accountable against our charter and charitable objectives, values and ethos" (Governance Document). Relatedly, a new, smaller board of 13 trustees was formed and the CEO gained trustee status and the ability to attend the nominations sub-committee, which identifies individuals for key positions including President, Chairman (sic.), and members of the trustee board. Notably, the representational group's primary formal mechanism to hold the Board of Trustees to account was through the instigation of an Extraordinary General Meeting (EGM) at which a vote of no-confidence can be raised. As my fieldwork came to a close, the CEO was proposing to remove this group's ability to pursue this action.

In terms of the nature of work undertaken to implement these governance structure changes, and in a similar vein to the co-optation of external experts explored in Chapter 3, an internal actor responsible for managing the process described the use of an "independent voice" to validate the need for change:

> "Although it was never publicly stated, the internal messaging was 'we know what the problems are, but if we as the staff tell the Trustees, they're going to not accept any of it …' I think at that time we weren't bold enough to say we know what the problems are and here they are. We wanted a third party to come along and say … here is what the problem is and here are some of the solutions that you might consider. If you get a well-respected, independent expert to come and say yes, these are your problems; that transfers that role to somebody else in a safe way. You've got an independent person coming in and saying 'this is how it looks to us' and it's more acceptable getting that message from a stranger who was looking at it cold. And that was quite interesting, but we already knew what the key result was going to be before we saw it."

When discussing the motivation for governance changes, colleagues persistently cited the ideology of the new CEO "thinking that the decision-making structure wasn't autonomous enough [for them]" … My view is that they are more of a commercial kind of person who wouldn't perhaps embrace ... what ... they see as red tape and things to stop them doing the things they want to do." They resent the "intrusion" and believed existing structures were "dysfunctional, leading to a kind of paralysis" that could be fixed by "something that looks much more like a conventional business." A senior manager provided the following account:

> "Suddenly the pace quickened ... Mainly [due to] getting into the corporate market [because of] the new CEO having a completely different ideology. That was ... the market that they understood ... And I think as the business grew ... there was greater need for more formality in how we did things around here and a whole lot more professional ... I think [they] certainly wanted a higher calibre of people on the Board. I mean, don't forget Carole, we went from a trustee of 40-odd people, and the majority of these ... We kind of inherited them as they were voted on by members. Whereas [current CEO's] approach was to select people who are more rounded and are more business people I think. You know, so you've got big business people."

In this narrative, the former democratically elected trustees are positioned as being more representative of the profession and thus the association but of "lower calibre" than "big business people." Notably, each change to governance structures served to reduce the number and power of stakeholders to which the CEO was accountable, further increasing their autonomy and ability to operate like a commercial entity:

> "There was a further dimension in that [these changes mean] your member element is transferred to being an advisory body. So, it has no powers whatsoever. It's purely advisory. So, it's the sounding board ... that's where we look if we want members' views. They have no ability, directly, through any sort of voting or other mechanism to influence what happens at the Board ... the direction to me was 'get rid of this huge body of Trustees, get me a small Board and a small Board made up of people who know what they're doing in business terms.' Business people was the phrase used, business people."

A number of governance characteristics that contravene the social, cultural and legal norms associated with charity governance, but that are commonly accepted within a corporate context, were instituted. Although it is common for the Chair of charity boards to take on some additional duties, such as line management of the CEO, the board is required in U.K. charity law to act collectively; the Chair has no more "powers" or authority than other trustees and cannot act in isolation. Yet the association's internal governance regulations position the Trustee Board as being "accountable to the Chairman of the Board as 'Head Trustee,'" placing that individual in a position of authority over the collective trustee body. Additionally, there was the matter of CEO–Trustee duality, which similarly contravenes Charity Law and requires special permission from the Charity Commission alongside revised Byelaws and Regulations within the organization not least due to the potential for conflicts of interest. My conversations at board level suggested a lack of awareness regarding the CEO's dual status, with one trustee displaying significant surprise:

> "I've never seen that before. I mean, I've never seen it before so it's genuinely not something ... I don't know how you're allowed to do that in best practice governance. I don't know ... They (CEO) are approving their own recommendations so, to me, you can't do that."
>
> **Carole**: So, when you have [CEO] at the Board, in what role do you see them?
>
> "They should be at the Board, but I thought they were there as a Chief Exec. I didn't know they were a Trustee. I don't receive them as a Trustee."

On discussing the rationale for CEO–trustee duality, a senior manager involved in the governance restructure noted:

> "... The internal logic, which wasn't the external logic ... was so that that trustee [CEO] could have a vote and ... if things were delicately balanced some Trustees would be highly influenced by the way in which that person voted. So, the sheep Trustees are going to wait and see how the chair of the Board votes and the CEO votes and vote according to that because they want to be seen to be good, sporting Trustees. I'm over simplifying this. They are not that passive by any means, but I think that's the sort of essential thought process."

The interplay between formal rules and informal practices was a recurring theme and came up again in relation to the nominations sub-committee, which deals with the selection of trustees, president and Chair. The formal governance regulations state that "the CEO will attend meetings of the Committee by invitation" but "shall not participate in shortlisting or voting, or recommending a preferred candidate, either for Trustees or for the Nominations Committee itself." The everyday talk within the organization, however, painted a picture of an "incestuous, old boys network," a "dark art, through the long list, the short list and the secret list" which "lacks safeguards, fairness and transparency":

> "It's a curious one because it can be quite incestuous and there aren't many safeguards in there ... So, the chief executive has an extremely powerful input to the selection process for the next chair. The next

> chair is the line manager of the CEO and will set their KPIs and remuneration and any bonuses that result. That, therefore, gives both parties a very strong vested interest in managing that relationship to both of their benefits. So, there's always a concern there. So, if you're a chair of the Board and your role up to now has been pretty inward looking, you actually want to make an external name for yourself and you wanted to do the next spread in a magazine, it's in your interest to give a favourable report to your CEO and approve their remuneration and approve any bonuses and give them a glowing testimonial. Quid pro quo. There are no checks and balances in that process."
>
> (Senior Manager)

A trustee reaffirmed this perception, remarking of the CEO: "[CEO] tells me they sit at the back [of the selection interviews] and say nothing … But they coerce … On the selection of the Chairman of the Board … so, it's a nice cosy arrangement isn't it. Yeah. Who's going to allow me [CEO] to prosper … well, it's you scratch my back and I'll scratch yours, isn't it?" In such circumstances, formal regulations and decision-making structures that are intended to prevent abuse and ensure "good governance" can be circumvented through informal power plays and covert trade-offs. Such actions, however, do not go unnoticed and can trigger contestation over role boundaries and authority. At a board meeting just before the fieldwork period ended, the trustees requested "The implementation of clear rules relating to the authority and voting rights of the CEO (in his/her capacity as a trustee) to avoid potential conflict of interest, specifically in the event of a split vote" (Minutes of Board Meeting, 2016). Other research we have been involved in has similarly pointed to nonprofits utilizing CEO–Trustee duality as a means to concentrate decision-making power in an elite sub-group and circumvent the collective decision making enshrined in charity law and codes of governance (Coule, 2015; Dick & Coule, 2020).

Senior Management: Increasing Power Distance and the Evolution of a Leadership Class

The distribution and negotiation of authority has been a key issue for organizations, and those who inhabit and study them, throughout the ages. In conventional Weberian-inspired accounts of organization, authority primarily derives from structures of hierarchy (Benoit-Barne & Cooren, 2009). Power is vested in someone by virtue of his or her office and associated with a line of authority or chain of command (Fayol, 1916; 1949) as well as legal or rational authority (Weber 1922; 1968). Power is therefore primarily managerial, residing with those who create, monitor and impose obligations (Perrow, 1986) – a leadership class if you will.

Major signals of membership in this class are managerial role titles and enhanced remuneration packages.

In 2014 the National Council for Voluntary Organisations (NCVO) undertook an Inquiry into Charity Sector Executive Pay, a subject that had come under scrutiny following some "high profile media articles into charity executive pay" (NCVO, 2014, p. 6). To set our discussion of the association in context, this report highlighted that less than 1% of U.K. charities employee *any* member of staff earning £60,000 or more. In the fieldwork period for this study, almost 11% of staff in the association earned £60,000 or more. Moreover, an analysis of remunerations of senior managers over a 5-year period (in which the employee headcount remained relatively static) shows some interesting trends in the development of a leadership class:

- The overall number of people earning over £60,000 per annum grew from 8 to 19;
- The number of people earning in excess of £100,000 went from 1 (the CEO) to 7;
- The CEO's remuneration package more than doubled;
- The pay differential between the CEO and next tier of management grew from in the region of £30,000 to £80,000.

Changes were also implemented to the bonus scheme, transforming it from a small payment of around £500 per individual regardless of salary grade, to one that disproportionately rewarded middle and senior managers. The changes resulted in employees in entry-level roles receiving a 31% increase, whereas middle and senior managers saw a 246% and 375% increase respectively. During the drafting process, the Head of Human Resources (HR) challenged the CEO's instructions in an email, stating:

> "[The proposal is] likely to disengage our staff by communicating a culture of elitism ... as the proposal would see circa £184k of profits go to 8 individuals and £132k going to the remaining 150 staff."

As part of this interaction, the head of HR presented an alternative proposal which – rather than exacerbating the leadership differential – looked to reduce it by freezing the leadership team scheme to fund the opportunity for other staff to achieve a bonus equal to 5% (rather than 3%) of their salary. On receiving the email from the head of HR, who reported to me at the time, the CEO came to my office and was angry to have been challenged regarding his decision and particularly in writing. The CEO's instruction was for me to tell her that this is "not the way we do things" and that she should go speak to the CEO directly on any future matters like this. When I chatted to the head of HR about the incident, she stated having deliberately sent the communication by email precisely to have her concerns formally on record. The CEO never responded to the head of HR's email. Soon after the incident she had a period of sick leave, eventually resigning from her role and citing cultural differences. The main point we wish to make, for now, is that the development of a leadership class within the association laid the foundation for a high power distance culture where employees accept the authority of senior role holders as natural and given (Hofstede, 1984; Hofstede et al., 2010) and if they can't, they leave.

Not only did remuneration for senior roles increase, the number of management roles increased through the introduction of a new tier of "middle managers." The number of director-level roles remained static, but their focus was reshaped towards growth and profit generation in line with the strategy discussed in Chapter 4. Table 5.1 summarizes the Director roles in the association during the former and incumbent CEOs' terms of office. Four things are particularly noteworthy – first, the intensification of attention, effort and investment towards corporate delivery (demonstrated by the move from one director overseeing sales and delivery to this market, to two directors – one for sales and one for delivery) and away from "governance"; second, the repositioning of knowledge as a commodity to be marketed and sold to consumers through the bookshop rather than the foundation for setting standards for the profession and syllabus development; third, the positioning of membership as a vehicle to serve the growth of the association; fourth, the emphasis on increasing global footprint through international growth. Points three and four were discussed in greater detail in Chapter 4.

Rationality, Gender and Emotion

Gender is entrenched in how work is organized, rewarded and experienced; it shapes social relations and behaviours at work and is embedded into the workplace itself (see Powell & Graves, 2003; Goodman, 2010 for general overviews of gender and work). Gender pay disparities and underrepresentation of women in senior executive positions within the corporate world are well documented, despite firms with a larger share of women in senior positions performing better, particularly in knowledge-intensive industries or those that employ more women in the labor force (Christiansen et al., 2016). In a sector dominated by female workers and suggested to prioritize wage equality, it is surprising that recent evidence suggests men continue to earn more than comparably educated and experienced women and that pay disparities can actually be bigger in some nonprofit fields (King & Lewis, 2017).

Within the association, four senior managers (including myself) survived the transition from the previous to the new CEO; two female, two male. The new CEO enhanced this senior team with the appointment of

Table 5.1 Summary of director roles in previous and incumbent CEOs' terms of office

Director roles under former CEO	*Director roles under incumbent CEO*
Director of HR and Administration Responsible for Human Resources, the post room and facilities management	***Director of Capability Development*** Responsible for HR, ICT, facilities management, post room, procurement and organization development initiatives
Finance Director Responsible for finance, procurement and ICT	***Finance Director*** Responsible for finance*(ICT and procurement move to Director of Capability Development)*
Director of Governance Responsible for compliance with Charity Law and regulation as well as Institute's own governing documents	No equivalent role
Director of Membership and Education Responsible for development and assessment of qualifications against standards developed by Professional Practice and Knowledge team and building the capacities/capabilities of the membership	***Director of Education*** Responsibility for development and assessment of qualifications. *(Membership moves to Director of Marketing, Membership and Knowledge)*
Director of Professional Practice and Knowledge Responsible for developing the "body of knowledge" for the profession and associated standards, plus the sponsorship of professorial appointments within the field	No equivalent role
Director of Marketing Responsible for supporting and promoting brand development relating to membership and education, and professional practice and knowledge activities	***Director of Marketing, Membership and Knowledge*** Responsible for brand, growth of community and membership and bookshop.
Director of Sales and Corporate Relationships Responsible for selling and delivering qualifications to corporations	***Director of Sales*** Responsible for sales to corporations ***Director of Corporate Delivery*** Responsible for delivery of qualifications to corporations
No equivalent role	***Director of International*** Responsible for setting up overseas offices, initiatives and projects

three further posts, one of whom was female. The final composition of the senior team, including the CEO, was 5 men and 3 women. The 3 female senior role holders all earned less than their male counterparts and the two men brought in by the CEO earned more than the two that pre-existed the CEO's term of office. Subtle underlying or systemic social norms and structures of power that (re)produce gender-based inequalities within the association included the expectation that female members of the team would minute the leadership team meeting, if the CEO's Personal Assistant was unable to attend. Not once in 7 years did I ever witness a male colleague being asked (or offer) to undertake this task; nor did my female colleagues, or indeed I, feel able to decline outright. There were a few occasions where I adopted serious humor and said "Oh, I guess it's my turn again then," to no avail. Social Role Theory highlights that leaders simultaneously occupy organizational and gender-defined roles and that women may be penalized for violating the latter in work contexts (Nicholson-Crotty, 2006). Perhaps this subconsciously played into our acceptance and indeed reproduction of stereotypic, gendered behaviour that undermined our "peer" status – see Bass (1990) and Eagly & Johannesen-Schmidt (2001) for informative accounts of how organizational culture and structure accentuate or obscure differences between male and female managers.

In a number of leadership team meetings, I witnessed and experienced male members of the team devote significant time and effort to provoking female colleagues to react emotionally. This was usually so their rationality could be challenged and used as a reason to discount their opinion in decision-making on the basis that they are "too emotional" – a gendered discourse of vulnerability associated with weakness (see Locke, 2011). My early military training had taught me that people could use my own emotions as a weapon against me, and that taking emotion out of my delivery meant the message itself would remain centre stage. Having been socialized into a leadership role within a male-dominated environment that valued the exemplification of dominance, control and assertiveness – assumed masculine traits – I had developed significant capacity for emotional control, which flies in the face of gender-linked stereotypes (Fabes & Martin, 1991; Shields, 2000). There was one male colleague in particular who would occasionally try and "bait" me in leadership team meetings and get incredibly and visibly frustrated himself when he could not sense a reaction; the boardroom really can be an emotional war zone.

Such behaviours were new and seemed to enter with and be further exacerbated by the corporatization of the association. What was interesting to and for me, was that my readings on ethnography and developing identity as an ethnographer brought my own "Otherness" as a manager into sharp focus. Just as reflexive ethnography attempts to break with the patriarchal, linear, disembodied nature of much (social) scientific writing

(Burrell, 1997; Höpfl, 2000), it also served in this case to reveal what lurks under the masculine-scientific surface of management. Rather than simply studying the association through and by means of my personal professional experience and identity (Tienari, 2019), the hyper-reflexive stance associated with autoethnography that simultaneously focuses on inward and outward observation (Kempster & Stewart, 2010) brought new (and unsettling) understandings to my identity and work as a manager.

References

Alves, I. (2009). Green spin everywhere: How greenwashing reveals the limits of the CSR paradigm. *Journal of Global Change and Governance, 2.1*, 1–26.

Bass, B. M. (1990). *Bass & Stodgill's Handbook of Leaderhip: Theory, Research, and Managerial Applications* (3rd Edition). New York: Free.

Benoit-Barne, C., & Cooren, F. (2009). The accomplishment of authority through presentification: How authority is distributed among and negotiated by organizational members. *Management Communication Quarterly, 23*(1), 5–31.

Burrell, G. (1997). *Pandemoniums: Towards a Retro-Organizational Theory*. London, UK: Sage.

Christiansen, L., Lin, H., Pereira, J., Topalova, P., & Turk, R. (2016). Gender diversity in senior positions and firm performance: evidence from Europe. *IMF Working Paper, WP/16/50, International Monetary Fund, Washington DC.*

Coule, T. (2015). Nonprofit Governance and Accountability: Broadening the Theoretical Perspective. *Nonprofit and Voluntary Sector Quarterly, 44*(1), 75–97.

Crilly, D., Zollo, M., & Hansen, M. (2012). Faking it or muddling through? Understanding decoupling in response to stakeholder pressures. *Academy of Management Journal, 55*(6), 1429–1448.

Dick, P., & Coule, T. (2020). Non-compliance with regulatory codes in the nonprofit sector: Accountability and the discursive coupling of means and ends. *Business and Society, 59*(4), 749–786.

Eagly, A. H., & Johannesen-Schmidt, Mary C. (2001). The leadership styles of women and men. *Journal of Social Issues, 57*, 781–797.

Fabes, R. A., & Martin, C. L. (1991). Gender and age stereotypes of emotionality. *Personality and Social Psychology Bulletin, 17*, 532–540.

Fayol, H. (1949). *General and Industrial Management*. London: Pitman (Original work published 1916).

Goodman, J. (Ed.). (2010). *Global Perspectives on Gender and Work: Readings and Interpretations*. Lanham, MD: Rowman & Littlefield.

Hofstede, G. (1984). *Culture's Consequences: International Differences in Work-Related Values* (2nd Edition). Beverly Hills, CA: SAGE.

Hofstede, G., Hofstede, G. J., & Minkov, M. (2010). *Cultures and Organizations: Software of the Mind* (3rd Edition). New York: McGraw-Hill Education.

Höpfl, H. (2000). The suffering mother and the miserable son, organizing women and organizing women's writing. *Gender, Work and Organization*, 7(2), 98–105.

Kempster, S., & Stewart, J. (2010). Becoming a leader: A co-produced auto-ethnographic exploration of situated learning of leadership practice. *Management Learning, 41*(2), 205–219.

Kerr, C. (1963). *The Use of the University*. Cambridge, MA: Harvard University Press.

King, C., & Lewis, G. B. (2017). Nonprofit pay in a competitive market: Wage penalty or premium? *Nonprofit & Voluntary Sector Quarterly*, *46*(5), 1073–1091.

Laufer, W. S. (2003). Social Accountability and Corporate Greenwashing. *Journal of Business Ethics*, *43*(3), 253–261.

Locke, A. (2011). The social psychologising of emotion and gender: A critical perspective. In W. Ruberg & K. Steenburgh (Eds), *Sexed Sentiments: Interdisciplinary Perspectives on Gender and Emotion* (pp. 185–206). Amsterdam, Netherlands: Rodopi.

NCVO. (2014). *Report of the Inquiry into Charity Senior Executive Pay and Guidance for Trustees on Setting Remuneration*. London: National Council for Voluntary Organisations.

Nicholson-Crotty, J. (2006). Gender roles, workforce composition, and management style: Female commanders and policy decisions in police organizations. *Working Paper. University of Missouri, Columbia USA*, 1–28.

Nyilasy, G., Gangadharbatla, H., & Paladino, A. (2014). Perceived greenwashing: The interactive effects of green advertising and corporate environmental performance on consumer reactions. *Journal of Business Ethics*, *125*(4), 693–707.

Pache, A., & Santos, F. (2013). Inside the hybrid organization: Selective coupling as a response to competing institutional logics. *Academy of Management Journal*, *56*(4), 1–63.

Perrow, C. (1986). Economic theories of organization. *Theory and Society*, *15*, 11–45.

Powell, G. N., & Graves, L. M. (2003). *Women and Men in Management* (3rd Edition). Thousand Oaks, CA: SAGE.

Shields, S. A. (2000). Thinking about gender, thinking about theory: Gender and emotional experience. In A. Fischer (Ed.), *Gender and Emotion: Social Psychological Perspectives* (pp. 3–23). Cambridge: Cambridge University Press.

Tienari, J. (2019). One flew over the duck pond: Authoethnography, academic identity, and language. *Management Learning*, *50*(5), 576–590.

Weber, M. (1968). In G. Roth & C. Wittich (Eds), *Economy and Society: An Outline of Interpretative Sociology*. New York: Bedminster (Original work published 1922).

6 Rewarding Loyalty to the (New) Cause

> "Increasing profits although required for [known liabilities] and growth investment, should morally go to staff making the growth ... [the association] is a business as well as a charity and must attract the best talent to sustain its strong growth. Our charitable status does not allow equity in the business through share options" (CEO, Pay and Reward Policy)

Inciting Individualism and Incentivizing Commerciality

As someone who started their career as a HR professional in the military, responsible for the implementation rather than design of pay and reward structures and schemes, I have to confess to having held a rather simplistic view of them; until analyzing them as an (albeit embedded) ethnographer. In this chapter, we narrate changes to the pay and reward scheme in the association over an extended period, portraying them as a vehicle to socialize, negotiate and embed particular organizing logics. In other words, they are an example of how management systems are reflective of the assumptions of those who create them (Argyris, 1973; Davis et al., 1997). Over a 7-year period, the incumbent CEO instigated a number of key changes to the pay and reward system. The introduction of pay scales and bandings, which created high power distance in pay and reward schemes and an exponential increase in the total salary bill of the association, was discussed in Chapter 5. We also drew attention in Chapter 4 to how achieving a "great" rating through performance review – which triggered up to an extra 5% bonus for the individual – was predicated on economic results. Here, we focus specifically on how the changes to the bonus scheme were designed to incite individualistic, commercially orientated behaviours through changes to the performance criteria.

Prior to the incumbent CEO's term of office, the association operated a modest, collective bonus scheme that was driven by and rewarded behavioural criteria such as ethics and respect, working practices, customer care and quality. Symbolically, this elevated the importance of the *means* by which we achieved organizational goals. The scheme was seen by an external pay and reward specialist to represent "a small thank you" to all staff for effective teamwork throughout the year. The actual payment of the bonus occurred in the December pay "to help people buy the turkey and trimmings for their family Christmas," invoking familial connections within the association. Eight years later the scheme had been re-designed to incorporate significantly higher payments calculated on a percentage of base salary and based on individual performance and one criterion – net financial return. To further signal the primacy of financial performance as the *end* itself, the association introduced sales commission for those roles deemed to be linked most directly to revenue generation, increasing the total reward opportunity for sales roles by 20% more than any other role.

Table 6.1 summarizes these changes to the bonus criteria and its communication to staff. What is notable is that the modest, collective bonus scheme that privileged "how we do things" was informally communicated by the CEO in a face-to-face staff briefing as a personal "thank you" to staff, had no formal eligibility criteria but specified expected behaviours in great detail. In sharp contrast, the individualized, high-value scheme that had a single trigger of £26 million revenue was communicated through a formal policy and written communications from the Finance Director and CEO. The articulation of the scheme rules and eligibility criteria were lengthy and written in consultation with a lawyer.

In Chapter 4, we narrated how money had become the primary driver of organizational behaviour, imbued within the symbolic systems, rhetorical repertoire and formal strategy of the association. As this transformation permeated the reward and recognition system and making money became the end game itself, regardless of the means used to achieve it, I became more and more aware of what many would see as perverse individual behaviours. This included directors hoping learners would fail their exams so they would then transfer onto a new programme giving greater financial returns, and middle managers feeling there was no option other than to lower the standards for an award to secure more future sales with a Multi-National Corporation because of commercial pressures. When discussing the purpose of the association, one of my director-level peers remarked:

> "We are measured, we are rewarded on certain metrics. So, you know, sales revenues are clearly an important one. So, there are some things that I do purely because there's some revenue there."
> **Carole:** "Important to whom?"
> "For [the association]."
> **Carole:** "Okay."
> "Okay. And to me, for my bonus. But they're important to [the association] because we need to grow the corporate revenue line."

Table 6.1 Bonus criteria and communication to staff

Previous CEO	*Incumbent CEO*
Communicated by CEO verbal update at bi-monthly staff briefing and supported by a printed handout	Communicated through the Pay and reward policy on internal intranet[1], Finance Director update at quarterly staff briefings and final bonus payment communicated by CEO at December end of year staff briefing
Achievement of the following objectives by all staff will trigger a bonus payment of £150 per person. The criteria are based around several areas relating to the institute's targets and how we need to operate to achieve those goals.	These Scheme rules are for guidance & are non-contractual. They replace in their entirety the previous rules & guidance regarding the payment of bonuses as set out in the document 'Global Pay & Bonus Policy' [The association] may in its absolute discretion pay staff a bonus of such amount, at such intervals & subject to such conditions as may in its absolute discretion determine from time to time. Any bonus payment to staff shall be purely discretionary & shall not form part of the employee's contractual remuneration. If [the association] makes a bonus payment to staff in respect of a particular financial year, it shall not be obliged to make subsequent bonus payments in respect of subsequent financial years.
Eligibility	
Section not covered	Eligible staff for the FY15–16 non-contractual bonus must meet the following criteria: • Employees on permanent or fixed term contracts, and; • Rated as at least good at the end of year appraisal for the qualifying period, and; • Who were on the payroll during the qualifying period, and; • Who are on the payroll at the time that any bonus payments are made even if they are not currently at work due to maternity, sick or some other approved absence.

(*Continued*)

Table 6.1 (*Continued*)

Previous CEO	*Incumbent CEO*
Performance Standards **Work ethics & respect** • Respect & understanding for all work colleagues, providing support & advice wherever possible, without the need for management prompting • No-blame method of working with colleagues – no rivalry or disrespect between teams • Accept responsibility for quality of output & quality of relationship with colleagues • Language & behaviour to all colleagues to be professional & respectful at all times • Standard of dress & personal appearance to be smart & professional at all times • Demonstrable understanding & acceptance of different cultures, personalities & beliefs – accept & respect petioles differences • Understand that whilst entertaining & socializing either with customers or work colleagues that you still represent as an organisation. **Working practices** • Constant interface with colleagues in cross-functional groups to ensure efficient & best use of resources • Self-motivated involvement in seeking & sharing information • Adhere at all times to institute polices & procedures • Proactively seek information – don't wait to be told • Abide by the principles of Ethical code in all dealings with suppliers	The table below provides the summary of standards that must be met to trigger bonus payments. **Activity** **Target** Revenue £26 million End of document

(*Continued*)

Table 6.1 (*Continued*)

Previous CEO	*Incumbent CEO*
• Abide by the requirements of the various business principles & practices • Understand the risk mitigation process & procedures & bring risk management to the forefront of your minds • Customer care & quality (The word customer is used as a generic term & refers to everyone for whom you provide a service – internal colleagues, customers, members, suppliers etc.) • Meet the needs of our customers in a high quality & professional manner • Treat all customers equally • Provide a 'corporate' image to all our customers representing the whole of [the association] at all times, not just one particular part – we must all act as Ambassadors cross-functionally • Go 'the extra mile' to ensure customer satisfaction – demonstrate commitment to the 'customer first' philosophy • Recognise that systems & procedures – as they are enhanced & designed – are there to assist customer care. Do not try to fit customer service provision around our systems/processes • Be aware of the need to 'manage' distressed or frustrated customers in a sensitive manner • Ensure you understand the variety of engagements a 'customer' may have across the whole of the institute & keep colleagues informed	

(*Continued*)

Table 6.1 (Continued)

Previous CEO	*Incumbent CEO*
Use of ICT • Effective use of systems – ensuring they are used as business tools as well as an operational system • Maintain quality data & take 'ownership' of the data on systems • Activity contribute to enhancements & the development of systems • Consultation about data collection & the use of data before making commitments – no 'independent' databases • Continued commitment to enhancing & growing our IT network & infrastructure • Actively follow & support the various IT polices & procedures to maximise the efficiency of the systems • Consult & include the IT team prior to developing/enhancing/changing business processes in your own area • Use of the telephone system as an aid to customer service – not as an aid to easier working at [location removed] • Maintain familiarity with the content & layout of the website – understand & maximise the benefits of using the website as an internal source of information & business information tool • Contribution to the website, with strong commitment to keep the website at the forefront of the brand image • Actively utilize & support the development of the intranet, ensuring information is relevant & useful. Ensure your accept responsibility for keeping the intranet up to date & relevant	

Table 6.1 (*Continued*)

Previous CEO	*Incumbent CEO*
Financial • Abide by the requirements, policies & procedures relating to the Institutes financial transactions • Consult with the Finance Team before committing to contracts with differing payment terms • Actively support the Institutes efforts to reduce debtors days by strong client management • Maximise savings & proactively think about the cost of doing things before going ahead (i.e. do you need a colour copy?) • Manage wastage – both staff time & materials	
Marketing • Commitment to supporting the brand image in the market place • Commitment to supporting the Corporate image & style in all correspondence/printed matter/ presentations style. Help colleagues, particularly those new to understand & abide by these rules • Active consultation with the Marketing Team at the initial stages of a project to utilize the expertise appropriately	

Source: Bain (2017).

The former CEO captured how *what* is measured acts as a powerful reference point for the interpretation of purpose, encouraging organizational inhabitants to prioritize behaviours and practices towards that end:

> "I felt after I left that [the association] lost its way a bit in terms of understanding that the commercial measures weren't an end game, but were a means to an end, and that … [It] started to become a more commercial organisation. There's nothing wrong with being

commercial in the sense of being business-like. There is something wrong with being commercial if commercial becomes the end game. So, you know, "aren't you a good boy; I'll give you a huge, great big bonus because you made a load of money this year". If you get what we're here for wrong then you measure the wrong stuff. So if a CEO's bonus is totally on, you know, we made two million quid this year but our reputation's crap and we haven't improved methods and all that stuff, in my view that's driving the place in the wrong direction. One of the worries I have about measurement, and that links to bonuses and staff appraisals and all that stuff, is if you don't go right back to what we're here for you can start measuring the wrong stuff, start rewarding people on the wrong stuff, and then you change that dynamic between what the place is for and what people think they're there to do."

Searching for a Referent Comparator for Pay and Rewards

There are various schools of thought when it comes to pay and reward patterns of nonprofit organizations. One view is that employees will accept below-market pay in exchange for (more) meaningful work within purpose rather than profit-driven organizations. Correspondingly, nonprofits sometimes intentionally underpay in an attempt to attract only highly motivated individuals who are committed to their cause (Rose-Ackerman, 1996; Handy & Katz, 1998; Benz, 2005; Borzaga & Tortia, 2006). An opposing view is that nonprofits overpay due to an absence of (profit-related) incentives to suppress pay-levels, such as shareholders, corporation tax and the like, and can direct surpluses to members or users (through lower-cost, higher-quality services) and employees (through higher pay) (Holtmann and Idson, 1993; Schumacher, 2009). Questions of pay in nonprofits are important because they tend to have higher turnover of staff, and low pay is cited as one of the most common reasons for leaving, because wage inequality reduces job satisfaction and because intrinsically motivated employees care more about wage equity (King & Lewis, 2017).

As mentioned in Chapter 5, the National Council for Voluntary Organisations (NCVO) waded into this debate in 2014 by undertaking an Inquiry into Charity Sector Executive Pay. The inquiry followed high-profile media attention to executive pay in U.K. charities and aimed to explore: the relationship between salary levels and public trust and confidence in charities; the arguments about what the appropriate levels of pay are for charity senior executives, and; how these levels should be arrived at. The outcomes of this report included "definitive guidelines for charity trustees" and the findings were endorsed by the U.K. charity regulator – The Charity Commission. The following are some of the noteworthy principles and recommendations published from this inquiry that are relevant to our discussion (NCVO, 2014, pp. 4–10):

1 Charity law binds organizations registered as a charity (and thus the association) and is firmly founded on certain values. Central to those is the requirement of exclusive public benefit.
2 All charities accordingly share some common characteristics that must be observed by trustees when they consider pay. They must be completely independent in formulating their policy and decisions, and their decisions must be reached solely based on the best interests of the charity and its beneficiaries.
3 Trustees exemplify the voluntary nature of the charity and are thus themselves unpaid, except in the rare cases where remuneration is authorized. As discussed in Chapter 5, the association obtained special permission/dispensation for the CEO to hold dual status, allowing both high-level remuneration in their executive role and a stronger opportunity to influence governance-level decision-making (contravening point 2 above).
4 There were four main viewpoints on charity executive pay, "all of them strongly held and vigorously expressed":

    a nobody who works for a charity should ever be paid;
    b pay for a small, top tier of managers is acceptable provided as many other people as possible are volunteers;
    c working for a charity is a special vocation and salaries are subject to a "charity discount," making them lower than comparable roles in other sectors;
    d charities should be well run on efficient business lines – and if that means high pay at the top, then so be it.

The incumbent CEO echoed this fourth viewpoint in the extract from the Pay and Reward Policy that opened the chapter, stating that as a "business" there was a need to remunerate highly to attract and retain the best talent to sustain growth. In reality, it went far beyond this. Prior to the incumbent CEO's term of office, the association had no formal pay policy. Following some questionable decisions relating to pay and bonus by an interim CEO, the board instituted a sub-committee with the following remit:

- Review and approve [the association's] employee remuneration policy for relevance and appropriateness;
- Review and set the remuneration package for the [association's] CEO, including any bonus scheme;
- Review and approve the CEO's recommendations for the remuneration of the Leadership Team. (Sub-Committee Terms of Reference)

The new CEO developed and proposed the first formal pay policy, which was subsequently ratified by the Remuneration Sub-Committee of the board. A key aspect of defining the policy was to choose a referent group against which the association's pay bands would be benchmarked. It was decided that the referent group for management roles (in the U.K.) would be national charities, as the association competed nationally for management level roles. For non-management roles, we competed locally so the referent group was organizations in the region, regardless of sector. The major finding of this exercise was that administrative roles, representing a significant proportion of employees, were grossly underpaid. In response, the association triggered a re-alignment process.

A year or so after this exercise, the CEO presented a proposal to the Renumeration Sub-Committee for their personal salary to shift from a lower base, higher performance-related ratio to a higher base, lower performance-related ratio. The sub-committee's approval of this proposal created a misalignment between the CEO's base salary and the pay policy, leading to the CEO arguing that the comparator for the top position should be London SMEs; changing both the geographic and sector comparator. The sub-committee approved this recommendation.

On approaching the ceiling of this referent group, the CEO argued that the comparator should be London Medium Enterprises (MEs), due to the association's growth aspirations. Despite the association not meeting the criteria of ME in terms of staff or revenue, the sub-committee accepted the future-orientated "aspiration" argument and again lifted the ceiling for the Chief Executive's pay. Notably, the question of whether growth (in and of itself) was an appropriate aspiration or basis for reward was never debated. After moving beyond any legitimate or true referent group, the CEO switched tactics to increase their remuneration package and began arguing for increases in all (other) employees' base and performance related pay in recognition of their successes. If approved, it would shortly be followed with what I termed the "oh wait, me too" strategy, after seeing the pattern several times.

This felt disingenuous to me, not least because when the CEO was arguing for their personal reward package to be higher than the norm (and against a different referent group to the rest of the association) they cited exceptional and individual differences to their role. Once they had exhausted this approach and I was no longer able to offer a credible external benchmark for their pay, they switched to championing an increase for everyone else in the association (whose roles were still in tolerance with their respective comparators). On securing agreement, they argued for the same percentage increase to be applied to their package. Of course, a 2.5% increase on a six-figure salary costs the association considerably more than a 2.5% increase on a £20,000–30,000 salary.

As the director with oversight for HR, it fell on me to commission the annual salary review and make recommendations based on the pay-market analysis. For the association, this now consisted of a full large-scale review of salary bands every 5 years, supplemented by smaller-scale inflation-based reviews in the intervening years. Based on the outcome of these assessments, and as secretary to the remuneration sub-committee, I would then write and present the annual pay recommendations to this sub-set of the board. Without fail, the sub-committee accepted the recommendations for all staff year after year. Yet, they would always challenge the premise that CEO remuneration should be treated in the same way on the basis that the CEO's package already exceeded any benchmark. It was clear that some members of the sub-committee felt that applying inflation-related pay increases to the majority (who were within benchmark comparator pay bands) and not the CEO would go someway to addressing the disparity. Within the fieldwork period, there was significant frustration that the CEO's contract was such that the only scenario in which they could avoid an annual pay increase would be if the market review recommended against it (unlikely given the method was linked to inflation) or if the CEO was under-performing (against objectives they had themselves set and based solely on revenue generation). One trustee referred to this as "the CEO setting the homework and marking the assignment." I suspect that if these particular remuneration sub-committee members had a longer tenure-ship, they would have moved to change the CEO's contract. As their term is just 3 years and they only attend three sub-committee meetings, they had limited opportunity to first identify the issue and then redress it. Given the short timescales and the CEO's performance in terms of their growth manifesto, there was little appetite to "rock the boat."

I can say that these meetings, and my role within them, caused me a good deal of internal conflict and concern that my personal integrity was under threat. Money is not and never has been the primary motivator in my career. A perspective that both irritated and amused the CEO who often told me that I was "naïve in my belief that money was not the only motivator that people came to work for." As such, there would routinely be numerous conversations and drafts of reports in preparation for this meeting; a meeting where I had to argue the case for my line manager's pay increase and make recommendations I did not believe in. I was often embarrassed and aggrieved that the CEO would position themself as benevolent in seeking the best for staff, whilst at the same time knowing the primary motivator was self-benefit. I was insulted at the assumption that I – and the members of the sub-committee – could not see their strategy for what it was and uneasy that sub-committee members may perceive I was "on-board" with proposals regarding the CEO's remuneration package. There was also discomfort in my knowledge that my ability to "manage" this meeting "successfully" made me valuable to the CEO. I was in no doubt that this gave me some leverage when negotiating other operational matters with the CEO; leverage that I often used for what I felt was "the common good."

Nevertheless, it came with a sense of vulnerability and I did sometimes wonder what would happen to me, and my role, if the remuneration sub-committee had ever rejected my recommendations.

Morality and "Profit" Sharing: Blurring the Line

Nine years after their appointment, the CEO proposed a further development based on the notion of "profit sharing." Essentially, the "success" of the organization would continue to be judged solely on financial performance and based on three tiers – meeting budget, exceeding budget and individual "great" ratings. The main change resided in linking bonus payments to salary, disproportionately benefiting senior employees (also see Chapter 5), and sharing "profits" (technically surplus in a charity context) that exceed budget by placing 70% into the organization's reserves and 30% into paying staff bonuses, with no maximum cap on the value. As working examples:

- If £100,000 surplus was created, £70,000 would be put into reserves and £30,000 would be distributed to staff (as a percentage of their base salary);
- If £1millon surplus was created, £700,000 would be put into reserves and £300,000 would be distributed to staff (as a percentage of their base salary).

This enhanced scheme was, as we saw in the extract opening the chapter, the CEO's work around for the association's charitable status preventing share options for employees. Rather ironically, the argumentation for profit sharing within formal proposals and verbally was consistently imbued with a moral imperative through the notion that "It is fundamentally wrong for the organization to be making significant profits and not distributing some of these back to staff" (CEO). Within the context of a privately owned corporation, we might consider profit sharing for employees a prosocial behaviour. In the context of charity and charter status, however, the term "profit" is often alien, let alone positioning it as the organization's raison d'etre or distributing it to employees for their contribution to growth.

This proposal triggered unprecedented struggle and contestation within the association, which went beyond the issue of pay and brought the line between community and corporate logics into sharp focus. In the drafting process, the head of HR expressed significant concern about the negative impact the bonus scheme proposal may have on management credibility and perceptions of equity. In a communication to the CEO, she wrote:

> "As part of my remit I feel that it's important to make you aware that I believe we have strayed from your original intention for the bonus policy and believe that it is important that I bring this to your attention

> now. I fully support what you are trying to achieve and believe that 'sharing success' is a great message. However, I do not believe that the proposed arrangement as it currently stands will achieve this objective. Money is very emotive. Studies have clearly shown that staff look primarily at internal equity when assessing whether or not they feel they are paid, and treated, fairly. If we get this wrong, I am concerned that repercussions for the organisation could be both long term and serious and may ultimately affect the credibility of senior management."

Pay came under scrutiny again when, at its first meeting, the new Finance Sub-Committee of the board reviewed the previous year's annual accounts. As part of this review, questions were raised about the value of the salary bill, which had seen an £800,000 increase over a twelve-month period. A committee member, who worked in the charity sector, challenged this as being "high compared to headcount" and a request was made for a briefing to take place at the next meeting on how pay and incentivization was managed within the association. It was at this second meeting that the proposal for the bonus scheme was presented and met with much discussion. The Finance Sub-Committee members stated that they were unwilling to approve the proposal and requested it to be taken to the full board meeting the following month. I attended the board meeting and recorded the following notes in my field-note diary:

> "My first instinct is that there has been a lot of lobbying prior to the meeting and you can see that there is a divide between those that support the proposal and those that do not. It comes across as two conflicted teams – those that support the CEO and the proposal and those that support the Chair of Finance Committee; I feel as if the issue being discussed has become personal and that the Chair of the sub-committee does not trust the CEO or the Chair of the Board. There has been a lively conversation with most Trustees giving a view and some raised voices and waved hands as they spoke. This appeared to me, an emotive discussion broadly around two questions:
>
> a Is it appropriate that we should have a bonus scheme (at all)?
> b Are the bonus triggers (objectives) suitable?
>
> The phrase "Don't let the leadership set the homework and mark it themselves" was first mentioned by the Chair of the sub-committee. This expressed a view that it was the Trustees' role to test assumptions and ensure that the leadership team were not setting an environment up where it was easy to be successful – with an inference that it is possible to "dumb down" the objectives so that the maximum trigger would be achieved. Both the CEO and Chair of the board responded, showing their frustration and suggested that the Trustees "were

> showing a major lack of trust." One of the trustees responded that "this is not about a lack of trust but just a facet of good charity governance."
> Another trustee who is a lawyer by profession jumped into this conversation stressing that the trustees must not take things at face value and that they have personal responsibilities and must be led by good practice to mitigate the risks. They cited the very recent collapse of "Kids Company" as an example of "what could go wrong."
>
> At the very end of the conversation the Chair of the sub-committee referred to the pension paper and "un-sized pension liability" – it became apparent that this paper had not been circulated to the wider trustee group and some felt that this had been a deliberate omission. I am not sure if the timing of this point was deliberate – I think it may have been presented in a deliberate way almost to suggest a lack of openness and therefore a reason not to trust. It was defended by the CEO, saying "it was an operational matter" and would come to the trustees in due course.
>
> The conversation ended with the Chair of the board stating that they had made the decision to approve the bonus proposal and did anyone disagree. The Chair said that at the end of the day it was down to the trustees to decide "how we feel about the plan." They said "by all means take guidance from Finance Sub-Committee but in doing this we must recognise we have a competent set of people running [the association]" and that "we have a duty to question the leadership but also to trust them." In the end there was some grumbling, some trustees were overt in their support – one trustee asked for it to be recorded that "they were not in agreement"."

I discussed the situation with a long-standing colleague who related the "Trustees discomfort at the new bonus arrangements" as a "good illustration of the tension between what the Trustees think should be the end game and what the business leaders (well, most of them) think should be the end game." In that moment, my colleague brought it right back to the war between community and corporate organizing logics within the association, and how this was playing out in respect of pay and reward. She remarked that the CEO "strongly believes that financial success and financial reward is a major motivator, they bring that sensibility from their previous life, it is a strong driver for them personally, and it is shared by other Directors who have come from the same background." She continued by suggesting that those trustees who objected did so because the idea of "commercial-rate cash rewards for staff of a charity didn't sit well with their view of themselves as voluntary Trustees taking no reward for their services to the profession." She contrasted this with the trustees own business lives, where they would "feel no inhibitions about seeking maximum remuneration for their expertise. So, it is their sense of what kind of organisation [the association] is, and what its end game is, that conditions how they view the remuneration policy – not whether [the association] can afford it."

Having been successful in getting approval for this new bonus structure, but still seeking more, the CEO again looked to amend the bonus structure 2 years later with the introduction of Long-Term Incentive Plans (LTIP). LTIPs capture arrangements to reward a member of staff for hitting targets over an extended period of time. In the case of the association, the CEO wanted to introduce an LTIP for key executives (including the CEO) that would reward them with "shares" based on performance. These shares would be awarded in place of the annual bonus but would be of a higher value and could only be "cashed-in" after a 5-year period.

I was dismayed at being asked to develop an LTIP proposal – a feature of most FTSE 100 CEO remuneration – and make a recommendation to the Board of Trustees. Not only did this cut across several personal principles and beliefs, but also is impossible within the charitable form. The (legally enshrined) essence of charity is that there is no "private ownership" and that unpaid trustees act as stewards of the charity's assets. Additionally, even if it were legally possible I could not understand how share options could ever be seen as "legitimate" in the charity context, either by external constituent groups (e.g. members of the association, the profession, partner organizations, suppliers, etc.) or internal groups who had chosen to work for or govern the association precisely because it was "for purpose" rather than for profit. As an experienced HR Director, I was well aware of the flaws in LTIPs, including paying CEOs on metrics that encourage gaming (which had arguably already begun) for little benefit to performance. Such performance-related pay systems were receiving intense criticism in major U.K. media outlets in the context of corporate firms (see https://www.theguardian.com/business/2015/may/13/long-term-incentive-plans-for-bosses-damage-firms), let alone charities.

I was aware that the CEO was looking to retire in 5 years, coinciding with the typical duration of an LTIP, and suspected that the motivation for LTIPs was driven by a desire to maximize personal gain. When I challenged the CEO on this, suggesting that if this was about his personal plans then he should have a conversation with the Chair of the board rather than introducing a scheme, they defaulted to the tried and tested line: "it's not about me it's about getting the best for the staff." I found this attempt at a moral or pro-social justification distasteful in a context where the appropriateness of LTIPs for any staff is questionable, at best. At an individual level, I had many conversations at home about how, as a director, I would tell the CEO that I did not want to be part of any LTIP scheme; I knew it would be met with derision at my "naivety" and the implicit suggestion that it was "wrong." Nevertheless, it cut across my value system enough for me to speak with the external consultants the CEO wanted to co-opt as an external expert source to legitimize the approach and create structures to make it possible. They candidly advised me not to go "head to head" on the issue; to take the money and donate it to a charity of my choosing. This felt like a somewhat unsatisfactory compromise – it is not what members pay their fees for – and one that would have made me complicit in bringing in an illegitimate, self-serving, high-risk practice that I did not "want on my watch." For a number of reasons, it was not long after this that I chose to leave the association.

The central point we wish to emphasize is that the transformation of the organization's central purpose and organizing logic manifest in all aspects of the pay and reward practices of the association, rooted in assumptions of Homo Economicus (economic man) (Doucouliagos, 1994, p. 877). A fellow director reflecting on the different approaches to pay and reward between the former and incumbent CEOs commented:

> "[With the former CEO] This was very straight forward, [they] were an advocate of 'a fairs day's work for a fair dollar.' Recognition was equal to reward (although he seldom demonstrated much of this!). Pay the job as fairly as possible and check against market rates for parity was his watchword.
>
> [The incumbent CEO] on the other hand applied a more mercenary approach, believing everything/everybody had a price!! Reward was bounty for scalps, a great example of this philosophy was the bonus scheme they manged to negotiate with the Trustees for themself, along with a much higher salary for the job than was evident in the market. I can best define this difference as one of equity and balance against the other of grab as much as you can carry!"

Maximizing individualist behaviour and emphasizing personal goals over group goals and a short-term status orientation had become paramount (Davis et al., 1997). The association and its workers were now measured by their worth as enterprises and their capacity to compete (Foucault, 2008); the "enterprise culture" (du Gay, 1996) had become embedded in the discursive and behavioural characteristics of the organization (Sandberg et al., 2019). The struggles over this manifestation will be our major focus in Chapter 7.

Note

1 The intranet is a private computer network accessible only to an organization's staff.

References

Adler, P. S., Forbes, L. C., & Willmott, H. (2008). Critical management studies. *The Academy of Management Annals*, *1*, 119–179.

Argyris, C. (1973). Organizational man: Rational and self-actualizing. *Public Administration Review*, *33*(4), 354–357.

Bain, C. (2017). *Interplay of Intentions: An Ethnography of Institutional Work Within a Hybrid Organization*. Unpublished DBA Thesis. Sheffield Hallam University.

Benz, M. (2005). Not for the profit, but for the satisfaction? Evidence on worker well-being in non-profit firms. *Kyklos: Jahrbuch des Instituts fur Geschichte der Medizin an der Universitat Leipzig*, *58*, 155–176.

Borzaga, C., & Tortia, E. (2006). Worker motivations, job satisfaction, and loyalty in public and nonprofit social services. *Nonprofit and Voluntary Sector Quarterly*, *35*, 225–248.

Davis, J. H., Schoorman, D., & Donaldson, L. (1997). Toward a stewardship theory of management. *The Academy of Management Review*, 22(1), 20–47.

Doucouliagos, C. (1994). A note on the evolution of homo economicus. *Journal of Economic Issues*, *3*, 877–883.

du Gay, P. (1996). *Consumption and Identity at Work*. London: SAGE.

Foucault, M. (2008). In G. Burchell (Trans.), *The Birth of Biopolitics: Lectures at the College de France, 1978–1979*. New York: Palgrave Macmillan.

Handy, F., & Katz, E. (1998). The wage differential between nonprofit institutions and corporations: Getting more by paying less? *Journal of comparative economics*, 26, 246–261.

Holtmann, A. G., & Idson, T. L. (1993). Wage determination of registered nurses in proprietary and nonprofit nursing homes. *The Journal of Human Resources*, *28*, 55–79.

King, C., & Lewis, G. B. (2017). Nonprofit pay in a competitive market: Wage penalty or premium? *Nonprofit & Voluntary Sector Quarterly*, 46(5), 1073–1091.

NCVO. (2014). *Report of the Inquiry into Charity Senior Executive Pay and Guidance for Trustees on Setting Remuneration*. London: National Council for Voluntary Organisations.

Rose-Ackerman, S. (1996). Altruism, nonprofits, and economic theory. *Journal of Economic Literature*, *34*, 701–728.

Sandberg, B., Elliott, E., & Petchel, S. (2019). *Investigating the marketization of the non-profit sector: A comparative study of two non-profit organizations. Voluntas*, doi:10.1007/s11266-019-00159-8.

Schumacher, E. J. (2009). Does public or not-for-profit status affect the earnings of hospital workers? *Journal of Labor Research*, *30*, 9–34.

7 Immobilizing Resistance and Overcoming Dissent

> "They [Trustees] want to be thought of favourably by the CEO. If they have ambitions to do other things [be Chair of the board or President] they want to be thought of favourably. So, the CEO is extremely powerful. And I mean, [the CEO] obviously has the same influence with staff here ... People respond to [them] in exactly the same way. I've seen how it works ... So that's fine as long as the chief exec is doing the right thing."
>
> (Senior Manager)

Whistleblowing: Making Sure There's Nowhere to go

It seemed to us that a key aspect of ensuring control, power and authority resided at the (executive) apex of the organization involved minimizing the risk and potential impact of whistleblowing. Put simply, the term whistleblower is used to describe people who disclose their observation(s) of illegal or wrongful conduct in their workplace to either "higher-ups" in their organization, or to outsiders who are perceived to be in a position to help, including journalists, legal authorities or regulatory agents (Mansbach, 2009). Viewed from a political perspective, truthful disclosures of this nature have been likened to "parrhesia"; an act of truth telling practised in ancient Greece (Mansbach, 2009; Rothschild, 2013). Foucault (2001) framed parrhesia as a fundamental feature of Athenian democracy and a privilege granted to honourable citizens, bestowing the right to free and frank speech in public spaces, promoting public deliberation and speaking truth to power. Whistleblowing in the workplace is similar to parrhesia insofar as it is intended to create change in the decisions and actions of (often) more powerful actors (Mansbach, 2009). Some have argued that it may even act as a counterforce to the trend towards marketization of the nonprofit world (discussed in Chapter 1); by pointing to nonprofits' failures to live up to their social purposes, whistleblowers introduce a discourse that can return organizations to their original values and purposes (Rothschild, 2013).

If the key to understanding whistleblowing lies within the organizational context that produces (or suppresses) the willingness and motivation to expose some kind of wrongdoing, the structural changes to the association discussed in Chapter 5 become ever more salient. The discursive and structural (re)positioning of charity as "outside" the mainstream business has the potential to transform what might be judged as "wrongdoing" by organizational inhabitants – what is deemed right or wrong (morally and ethically speaking) is different in a charity to a corporate context. The direct measures to increase the CEO's influence over the board, such as their dual CEO–trustee status and "coercion" regarding Chair selection and the Chair's additional powers as "Head Trustee" was seen to result in an "old boys network" where favours are exchanged for mutual advancement in a quid pro quo type arrangement. The introduction of "high power distance" pay and reward systems and more "management tiers" served to deepen the hierarchy and distance between the leadership elite and "the managed." The removal of "board partners" where each director was paired with a board member increased the divide between executive and board leadership, so the CEO became the single point of contact between staff and trustees.

These contextual features of the organization may act to supress any potential willingness to expose perceived wrongdoing, as they foster an environment where organizational inhabitants may have little confidence that "higher-ups" would "do the right thing" in the event of a disclosure. I had experienced this myself in relation to changes to pay and reward systems generally and the negotiation of the CEO's remuneration package specifically (discussed extensively in Chapter 6). On becoming increasingly uncomfortable with the situation I began to test the water in my conversations with the then Chair of the Board (and subsequently their successor). The Chair of the Board was also the Chair of the remuneration sub-committee. There were numerous conversations where I stated very explicitly that, not only did the CEO's remuneration package surpass any charity-specific benchmark, but that it was also outside *any* suitable referent group. There were other times where I pointed out that the level of bonuses and the proposed use of long-term incentive plans in the association could be seen to contravene the social norms and expectations of charities and thus hold reputational and legitimacy risks. The Chair(s) never took up the subtly delivered but nevertheless significant issues I put in front of them. I therefore never really knew if it was "safe" to speak freely and frankly to the Chair(s) about what some might view as morally or ethically questionable pay and reward, and governance practices within a charity context. Consequently, that was as far as I pushed it. I recall a conversation with a long-term peer, Dee, where we talked about this exact topic. Dee was responsible for governance and compliance within the association for as long as I can remember:

Dee: "They [he trustees] are the check and balance, they're the watchman and … if you had a scenario you're thinking about whistleblowing, where would you go?"

Carole: "Yeah, we've had that conversation before. Where would you go Dee?"

Dee: "Where would I go? It should be the chairman of the board and I'm not sure I would."

Carole: "Because of their relationship with the chief exec … not because of who that person is, but literally the relationship?"

Dee: If I thought the company was carrying on really bad, really bad and … and I wasn't confident that they would do anything about it or they would seek to … just cover it up. I'm not sure I … at the moment, I would feel comfortable to go to the chairman of the board."

Carole: "Who, arguably is another puppet … glove puppet rather like the remuneration sub-committee?"

Dee: "Yeah. Yeah. But that might just be me. There aren't enough … there aren't enough walls between people. The checks and balances aren't really there, we've been saying they are, they aren't really there. So in some ways you do really need to ask … who is not going to be seduced by [the CEO], by … having nice drinks in London somewhere and having a chat and putting the world to rights. Someone who will actually stand apart and say I'm going to criticise this, and I don't care."

Revisiting the challenge made by the Head of Human Resources to the CEO's proposed changes to the bonus scheme (discussed in Chapter 6) as an act of parrhesia sheds further light on these dynamics. As her line manager, I experienced the Head of HR as highly principled with strong moral convictions, a high sense of personal efficacy and social responsibility. Interestingly, these are the characteristics research commonly attributes to those most likely to whistleblow (see Graham, 1986; Jos et al., 1989; Miceli & Near, 1992; DeMaria, 2008) and they shine through in her communication to the CEO:

> **From:** [Head of HR]; **To:** CEO; **Cc:** Carole Bain; **Subject:** Staff Bonus Scheme
> "Dear [CEO]
> Further to our meeting on Monday, the Staff Bonus Payment Policy is being rewritten as per your instruction. I will have the draft to Carole before I finish for my holiday on Friday.
> I would like to take the opportunity to rewind on this a little as I am concerned that the new proposed staff bonus arrangement, as discussed at that time, does not fit the purpose as intended. When

we first spoke about this, you clearly advised me that you wanted to introduce a scheme in which all staff get to share in the financial success of the Organisation. You advised me that you felt that it was fundamentally wrong for [the association] to be making significant profits and not distributing some of these back to staff. You felt that the current staff bonus scheme does not drive this ethos of sharing success. Through discussion we agreed that, culturally, creating a 3-tiered approach to the bonus scheme (Senior Management, Middle Management and remaining staff) would be likely to disengage our staff by communicating a culture of elitism. I therefore drafted up the numbers based on Senior Management remaining eligible to receive 10% of their base pay with the remaining staff eligible to receive 5% of their base pay. On hitting NFR [Net Financial Return] my recommendation was that senior management [Directors and CEO] arrangements do not change whilst the remaining pot is distributed evenly between all staff. In other words, a blended approach to the employee bonus scheme.

On Monday, you advised me that on hitting NFR, you want to reduce the all-staff bonus to 3.5% of their base salary and increase the senior management bonus from 10% to 15% of their base salary. For staff that are on Band E [the lowest pay grade] they will be no better off than with the current bonus plan in place. We have circa 20% of the global workforce on Band E with circa 17% on Band D who would receive an additional £235 gross over and above the current scheme, which would equate to a net payment of approximately £150.

As part of my remit at [the association] I feel that it's important to make you aware that, under this proposed new arrangement, 8 employees would have their pay increased by between £5,000-£10,000 each over and above the current bonus arrangement, whilst introducing a scheme in which 37% of the workforce would not really see any tangible benefit on hitting NFR. The new arrangement would see circa £164k of profits go to 8 individuals in this Organisation and £132k to the remaining 150 employees. I believe that we have strayed from your original intention for the bonus policy and believe that it is important that I bring this to your attention now. I fully support what you are trying to achieve and believe that 'sharing success' is a great message. However, I do not believe that the proposed arrangement as it currently stands will achieve this objective. Money is very emotive. Studies have clearly shown that staff look primarily at internal equity when assessing whether or not they feel they are paid, and treated, fairly. If we get this wrong, I am concerned that repercussions for the Organisation could be both long term and serious and may ultimately affect the credibility of senior management.

With kind regards

[Head of HR]"

We see in the above communication that the Head of HR took a cautious and respectful approach to the challenge, pointing to her agreement with the original intent for the changes to the scheme (as articulated by the CEO) and bringing it to their attention that things have strayed away from this intent (with potentially serious consequences). In doing so, she offered the CEO an opportunity to correct the course of action without "losing face." At the same time, she does not shy away from challenging the elitism that the proposed changes are founded upon and evokes notions of fairness and equity in making her case against the CEO's decision.

I would see her very much as an "ethical resister" (Glazer & Glazer, 1989) committing "principled organizational dissent" (Graham, 1986) in order to exonerate herself from or avoid being complicit in such conduct. It was an act of integrity, and at the same time an anti-hierarchical act. It said, "you may be my superior and the authority in this workplace, but I have the right to speak truth to power on behalf of my fellow employees." I think it was this challenge to authority (in writing and thereby traceable) that provoked an angry retaliation from the CEO. Did I give the Head of HR the dressing-down the CEO instructed – no. But nor did I have the courage to take this beyond the CEO, precisely because I had received no indication there was an appetite to address these kinds of decisions and behaviours; something with which I still have an internal struggle. My sense is that the retaliatory response, lack of corrective action and willingness to cover up her overt statement of perceived wrongdoing magnified her sense of her own integrity and moral correctness of her actions while leaving a deep-seated sense of distrust toward us – the senior managers in the association. Ironically, the Head of HR's previous employment experience prior to the association was in the corporate world, to which she returned soon after this incident. She was not inherently against the practices common within the corporate sphere per se but was unable to reconcile them in the nonprofit context where she perhaps expected a greater sense of egalitarian ideals, pro-social behaviours and civic virtue (King & Griffin, 2019). Indeed, organizational inhabitants show a willingness to go against charity norms if they believe it benefits the right people in the right way (Dick & Coule, 2020), but not in pursuit of self-interest within an organization that claims primarily to produce social good(s).

So, considering the unwillingness of senior actors to "receive" internal disclosures and take corrective action, what prevented potential whistleblowers from disclosing wrongdoing to outsiders? For Dee and I, who were long-term inhabitants of the association, several factors made the potential fall-out from that action – the destruction of the entire organization – ethically complex and ultimately too heavy to endure. First, we were deeply committed to the association's intended, original purpose, to which we believed it could return under different conditions. Second, we had wide-ranging personal, professional relationships with many colleagues. We had seen them "grow-up" (professionally speaking) within the organization, suffer bereavements and other forms of loss, get married, start families – families that would suffer significant hardship if the association were to be closed down. For organizations, relying on such emotional ties or social bonds to prevent whistleblowing is precarious; others may choose a different path in navigating such a dilemma, given the multiple systems of ethics that guide moral thought and action.

To illustrate, from a deontological perspective, encapsulated in the writings of German philosopher Immanuel Kant, ethical conduct arises from putting duty first. Duties are defined through rational thought and are owed to all human beings rather than specific to particular kinds of human beings. Deontologists argue that any rule of action should be universal (i.e. good for all persons at all times). To be universal, a rule of action must be consistent (acceptable to/works well for society as a whole and can be widely practised) and reversible (adheres to the "do unto others as you would have them do unto you" rule) (see Orend (2000) for a contemporary application of Kantian ethics). Following this line of thinking, our moral duty was to expose the actions of those individuals who were flouting the spirit, if not the letter, of charity law and regulation which represents a set of universal rules designed to serve society as a whole and be widely practised. But, what if disclosure (of the actions of one or two individuals) to the regulator threatened the livelihood and security of over 100 people and disadvantaged an entire global profession?

From an alternative standpoint of virtue ethics, founded upon the writings of the Greek philosopher Aristotle, ethical conduct arises from particular personal qualities or virtues. Aristotle advocated the ethical value of virtuous qualities such as truthfulness, courage, temperance, pride, generosity, gentleness/concern for others, friendliness, modesty, justice, righteous indignation and high-mindedness. Taking the sum of all the seemingly "small" contraventions relating to governance and management practices in the association, is there more value in the virtue of courage and truthfulness (to disclose to "higher ups" despite indications they would take no action or by choosing to disclose wrongdoings to the regulatory body) or in gentleness and friendliness (by caring about the implications for all our colleagues)? Which course of action would lead to the greatest "Justice?" Our point in briefly digressing into theories of ethics is that, whatever the guiding principle of action (moral duty or virtuosity), in the grey areas of organizational life whistleblowing is a complex ethical dilemma involving questions about what it means "to do what is right," rather than simple decisions of "right" and "wrong."

The Resistors: Waiting Them Out, Flushing Them Out

The reformed governance structures, processes and practices introduced in Chapter 5 resulted in significant "turnover" in the governing body. The tenure-ship for the Chair was 2 years (having had to serve a minimum of

1 year as a trustee before becoming Chair) and for trustees was 3 years. Moreover, one-third of the trustee body changed each year. Because of this rotation it was impossible for any trustee, other than the Chair, to be there for a full 3-year strategy cycle. The Chair could be present for a full cycle if they served a full 3 years as a trustee before being selected as Chair for a further 2 years, perhaps explaining the CEO's vested interest in Chair selection (see Chapter 5). Organizational strategy is important in the context of governance as it is one of the key mechanisms for the board to shape and agree the direction of travel, core activities and performance measures that will advance the organization's mission and by which they can hold the CEO and staff to account.

To illustrate the process "in action," in any given strategy cycle the board would consist of three groups. Group 1 would join at the start of the strategy setting process, which usually took approximately 1 year from start to finish, and have little knowledge of the inner workings of the association. In their first year they would be involved in developing the new strategy and monitoring progress against the final year of the previous strategy via an annual operating plan, which they had no involvement in or prior knowledge of. In year two they would oversee the first implementation year of the strategy they contributed to developing. In year three they would oversee the second implementation year of that strategy and associated annual operating plan. The introduction of annual operating plans in year two and three of any given strategy cycle was significant in that it became the reference document for board-level conversations, allowing "creep" in the focus and targets that were documented in the longer-term strategy. As this group are in their final year, however, there is limited time and opportunity to identify and challenge this.

Members of group 2 have been trustees for 1 year. In their first year, they had monitored progress of the second implementation year of a strategy they did not develop and associated annual operating plan. In year two, they see out the third implementation year of that strategy through a new annual operating plan and take part in setting a new strategy. In year three, they monitor progress against the first implementation year of the strategy they set and agreed.

Members of group 3 have served 2 years of their 3-year term. They have overseen the first implementation year of a strategy that was developed the year before they joined the board, followed by annual operating plans associated with that strategy in their second and third years. Their third year would also consist of developing the strategy that they will never oversee in terms of implementation.

Figure 7.1 visually depicts the relationship between the strategy and trustee tenure-ship cycles, demonstrating how no trustee group would ever develop and see through to completion a single strategy under current governance arrangements. Moreover, ten groups of trustees would be involved in just three strategies, rendering "corporate memory,"

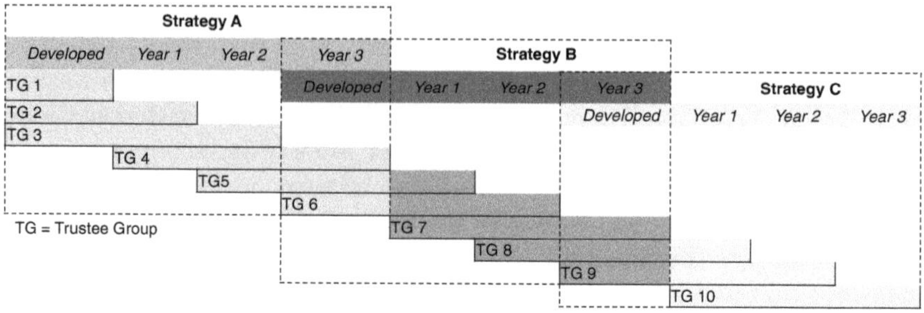

Figure 7.1 Strategy to trustee tenure-ship cycle.

continuity and ability to monitor medium–long term deviations from organizational purpose seriously problematic.

Towards the end of my period in the field, one of the trustees (featured in the final section of this chapter) who was coming to the end of her tenure, started to moot the idea that the CEO was "stalling" a governance review requested by the board in order to "wait them out," thereby avoiding a review that could thwart the CEO's power and authority. There is some support for this theory in the minutes of Board meetings where trustees challenged, requested reviews and changes to various governance structures and practices for over 2 years, which were never actioned.

In response, the trustees collectively started to push for the Chair's term to be extended from 2 to 3 years and for trustees to be able to serve two terms (6 years in total). The CEO resisted the proposed changes, perhaps due to short-term trustee tenure-ship being instrumentally valuable to them insofar as it limited the capacity for any individual or group of trustees to track the transformation of the association's ideological foundations and practices over an extended time-horizon. For example, returning to the changes to the association's reward scheme introduced in Chapter 5, and more extensively discussed in Chapter 6 we can see the CEO's establishment (consciously or sub-consciously) of an "edging strategy." What we are referring to is an approach that gradually erodes rather than dramatically breaks from the old and seemingly successful system and its associated practices. In other words, there was no big bold act, but rather the long-term introduction of apparently benign changes that eventually broke down previous boundaries and created space for new meanings and practices. By making small, incremental changes the incumbent CEO tested organizational inhabitant's readiness to adopt new approaches and naturalized such approaches over an extended timeframe while also reducing the potential for detection. Table 7.1 summarizes the gradual changes introduced to the reward scheme by the incumbent CEO over a 7-year period that constituted economic capital as the raison d'être of the association and the most appropriate reward for staff.

Table 7.1 Summary of reward scheme changes over 7-year period

CEO	*Year*	*Governance/ approver*	*1. CEO*	*2. Leadership team*	*3. Regional director*	*4. All staff (excluding 1, 2, 3 & 5)*	*5. Sales team*
Former CEO	0	**CEO**	**Collective bonus scheme in place** All staff bonus – linked to share of modest bonus pot. Payment dependent on 5 performance criteria, 1 of which is financial. Size of pot capped by a figure determined appropriate by the CEO.				
Incumbent CEO	1	**Pay Committee**	**New bonus criteria** – move from 5 criteria to financial surplus performance and customer satisfaction scores. All other details remain the same				
	2	**Pay Committee**	**Change to bonus scheme criteria.** All staff bonus – removal of customer satisfaction scores as performance criteria				**New Sales team bonus,** linked to revenue Capped to 40% of salary Cap determined by CEO
	3	**Pay Committee**	**Introduction of high power distance scheme, involving 4 tiers depending on job role**				No change
			Bonus capped at 33% of base salary Linked to	Bonus capped at 13% of base salary Linked to performance, 2 of 6 criteria being financial	25% of base salary linked to financial perfor-mance	Remain on previous scheme but addition of individual "great" performance	No change

(*Continued*)

Table 7.1 (Continued)

CEO	*Year*	*Governance/ approver*	*1. CEO*	*2. Leadership team*	*3. Regional director*	*4. All staff (excluding 1, 2, 3 & 5)*	*5. Sales team*
			perfor-mance, 2 of 6 criteria being financial			bonus linked to appraisal rating capped at 5% of base salary [cap determined by CEO]	
	4	**Pay Committee**	**New salary bands implemented**				
			No change.	Bonus cap increased to 20% of base salary.	No change.	No change.	No change.
	5	**Pay Committee**	No change	No change	No change	No change	Individual commission implemented
	6	**Finance Committee**	CEO tier removed and merged with leadership team but accompanied by increase in base salary commensurate with the reduction in bonus. No change to leadership tier		No change	No change	No change
	7	**Pay Committee**	**New scheme introduced** – 3 tiers based on: meeting budget, exceeding budget and individual great as before. Main change is the link to salary for all staff and the introduction of the enhanced payment – when financial results exceed targets the overachievement will be				

	"shared" 30% to staff and 70% to organization; 30% pot shared based on percentage of salary bill. Maximum value not capped		
	Meeting budget, 10% of base salary linked to 3 financial objectives Meeting enhanced budget, see earlier. Expansion of individual great eligibility to Leadership Team	Meeting budget, 3.5% of base salary linked to 1 financial objective. Meeting enhanced budget, see earlier	As per all staff (4) plus commission

Source: Bain (2017).

In addition to the creation of governance structures and processes that enabled dissenters to be "waited out," at other times there was a direct approach to "flushing out" the opposition.

Ronald worked at the association in a director-level role at the point the incumbent CEO was recruited. Shortly after the new CEO arrived, Ronald was "let go" through a redundancy process. There is a common notion in "business" circles that the recruitment of a new CEO is so costly that the first thing they must do is take measures to recoup this cost. The narrative within the association was that Ronald's redundancy was the new CEO's way of "paying for their [own] recruitment."

Several years later Ronald reappeared in the association having been nominated (i.e. democratically elected) to the board of trustees by the association's membership. He attended three board meetings as a trustee before stories of a "shout down" or "stand-off" between Ronald and the CEO, where Ronald had openly disagreed with and challenged the CEO started to circulate. Some colleagues felt this was "Ron's revenge" on a CEO who had let him go, others might argue that conflict is a natural, inevitable and sometimes productive aspect of organizational life (see Kassing (2000; 2008; 2009); Garner (2009a; 2009b); Goodboy et al. (2008) on the dynamics, triggers, risks and strategies of organizational dissent). A fellow director and good friend of mine felt that the CEO "saw Ronald as a threat partly because he had spilled the beans to [two trustees] concerning the unsuitability of the previous [short-lived] CEO, and current CEO feared there was a risk he might do the same about them. This paranoia carried on when Ronald was elected a board member. [The CEO] went to considerable effort to discredit and get rid of Ron, enlisting [several board members] in the detail of this."

Indeed, in an unprecedented response, the CEO rallied the trustee body to submit a vote of no confidence against an individual trustee, due to unacceptable conduct. This vote was subsequently brought into force by the nominations sub-committee and Ronald was removed from the board. Ensuring this situation could not arise again, the CEO instigated changes to the association's governance regulations to ensure no person employed by the organization could subsequently ever occupy the office of trustee. The CEO was a former board member turned executive of the association, who had then re-secured trustee status. In other words, they were flouting the very regulation they themself put in place by concurrently holding dual CEO–trustee status. As was shown in Chapter 5, however, not all trustees were aware of this dual status; again, likely made possible by the short tenure-ship of trustees.

"That Woman": Discrediting the Opposition

In Chapter 5 we introduced the trustee who was surprised to learn that the CEO was in fact also a trustee of the association. She had "never seen that before" and did not "know how you're allowed to do that in best practice governance" given that the CEO would be "approving their own recommendations so, to me, you can't do that." We also showed in Chapter 6 how the same trustee (referred to here as Vivienne), as Chair of the Finance Sub-Committee, started to introduce this "don't let the leadership set the homework and mark it themselves" narrative to mount a challenge to proposed changes to the bonus scheme within the board as a whole. This culminated in serious questions regarding unilateral decision-making between the CEO and Chair of the board, too much emphasis on commercial performance at the expense of "social goods" and a general neglect of "good governance" in relation to structure and processes.

Specifically, within the forum of the board Vivienne started to unpick and challenge the formal authority of the Nominations Sub-Committee. She requested "legal guidance to confirm the role of the [committee] in appointing Trustees and whether the Board had the power to block the recommendation from the committee and if so, on what grounds." This would be accompanied by "an Extraordinary Board meeting to which the Chairman of Nominations Committee would present an update detailing: (a) the process and procedure undertaken, and (b) the rationale behind the committee's decision to appoint each of the named individuals" (Board Meeting Minutes). Notably, the sub-committee concerned was one that the CEO was commonly known to "heavily influence" (see Chapter 5) and its Chair was seen as a "big buddy" of the CEO. Additionally, she requested "the implementation of clear rules relating to the authority and voting rights of the CEO (in their capacity as a trustee) to avoid potential conflicts of interest, specifically in the event of a split vote." (Board Meeting Minutes). Table 7.2 summarizes the governance structures, processes and practices that Vivienne homed in on during board meetings over a 2-year period, starting towards the end of her first year of tenure.

One of the very tangible, structural changes Vivienne brought about through the charges she levelled was the introduction of a new sub-committee to oversee the financial governance of the association – referred to interchangeably as the audit sub-committee or finance sub-committee. There was a perception among senior colleagues that the CEO had "shied away from [having an audit committee]" (Director) and "was resistant to the idea for a very long time. Their view was if we're a competent group of managers here, we shouldn't need one ... they didn't want them [the trustees] to be getting that deep into detail." (Senior Manager). One of the justifications for not having such a committee was that "we didn't have any qualified accountants or anything like that or anybody that had any accounting background to actually serve on those committees." As several colleagues went on to explain, that changed with the evolution of governance structures instigated by the CEO (and discussed in Chapter 5), perhaps with unintended consequences:

> "Now, of course that changed when we moved to a smaller Board and we got a higher calibre of people on the Board. And we then had

Table 7.2 Challenges to governance structures, processes and practices at board meetings

	Financial year 1				*Financial year 2*			
Meeting	*1*	*2*	*3*	*4*	*1*	*2*	*3*	*4*
Nature of challenge								
Need for greater transparency of trustee selection (Nomination Committees process, criteria and decision-making)	✓		✓	✓		✓	✓	
Clarity of process for electing chair of Nominations Committee						✓		
Challenge to the legality of Nominations Committee								✓
Rejection of proposal for a trustee							✓	
Challenge to the trustee selection process								✓
Request for extension of term of office for Board Chair from 2 to 3 years	✓	✓					✓	
Ability for Trustees to serve two terms of office	✓	✓				✓		
Concern of a disconnect between the Board and the member representation group	✓	✓				✓		
Challenging the time, it has taken to conduct a governance review								✓
The appropriateness of the CEO being a trustee as he had the potential to misuse his voting rights								✓

Source: Bain (2017).

the likes of qualified accountants. The … introduction of people like [Vivienne] onto the Board … I think at the end of the day they [the CEO] bowed down to pressure, but they could see the logic of having those people in … because it … they could deal with matters as a subset of the Board. We weren't then wasting the Board's time, Carole, in discussing audit issues, appraisal and all that sort of stuff."

[Director]

> "We wanted someone who was an expert in those areas who would take a critical look and advise us what we needed to do to get our act together. And that happened big time. [Laughs]."
>
> [Senior Manager]

There were numerous accounts of the CEO feeling "pressured" and "brow beaten" by "challenges at every turn" from Vivienne. So, why didn't she get the same treatment as Ronald? We think several conditions created a different set of dynamics that help to explain the lack of direct action to "neutralize" this opponent. First, she had no axe to grind; the absence of any previous relationship with the CEO or the association meant she could not be easily discredited as a disgruntled individual, bent on revenge.

Second, in the same way that the CEO had cultivated personal social ties with key people in positions of influence, she too had demonstrated long-standing allegiances with "significant people" in the board – namely the future Chair. It came to light in a finance sub-committee meeting that the two of them had attended university together many years ago and signalled that they had met prior to the committee meeting by arriving together (late) holding identically branded coffee cups. It was in this meeting that both the CEO and Chair of the Board accused Vivienne of bringing their integrity and competency into question.

Finally, as a Finance Director in a large U.K. charity herself, she "knew" charity governance. She regularly cited charity law, regulation and best practice alongside her experience as a trustee for a major children's charity at the time of the Jimmy Saville scandal erupted as examples of why trustees must take their role and responsibilities seriously. In doing so, she presented any challenge, not as a personal one, but as a matter of good governance; compliance with both the letter (of the law) and spirit (social norms and expectations) of charity. Indeed, at a board meeting I attended, the trustee rebutted the Chair's charge that she was displaying a lack of trust in the executive team by replying, "this is not about a lack of trust but just a facet of good charity governance." This position was consistently adopted throughout the trustees' tenure-ship in private and public fora and thus appeared genuine. In an interview conversation early in her term, I had asked Vivienne what, if anything, would make her leave the board (before her term ended). She responded with:

> "If the executive didn't listen to the feedback that the Trustees give. If I felt that my views weren't aligned with the other Trustees. I'm not commenting on who's right and who's wrong. For me, if I was seriously concerned about the risk and infrastructure of the charity and their ability to honour their charitable status."

Her expertise served to raise awareness of and gave her legitimacy as an advocate or guardian of good governance among other trustees from non-charity backgrounds. In one heated discussion, a fellow trustee who was a lawyer by profession reinforced her message, stating that the "Trustees must not take things at face value and that they have personal responsibilities and must be led by good practice to mitigate the risks" (Fieldnote Diary). Many of these exchanges resulted in board-level requests to review several aspects of governance in the association.

The CEO and Chair were by no means passive recipients of the challenge to their authority and integrity, propagating a narrative among senior staff members that Vivienne was "frightening the other Trustees into doubting themselves, doubting whether or not they were equipped to have the oversight role that they're supposed to have" and "undermining [internal] staff ... So, by saying constantly 'I'm a finance expert' and 'I'm looking at this and I'm telling you it's not being done properly,' that's quite a powerful statement to make" (Senior Manager). The Chair was more pointed, positing that Vivienne "scare mongered the Board, who were previously quite content with the ratification of the accounts ... I observed [Vivienne] using their advanced knowledge of charity law, compared to the other Trustees, to create a burning platform and a position of fear." His account then took an increasingly personal turn, stating that Vivienne's "whole persona was the antithesis of [the CEO's]. And that was the problem. It was a clash." But a clash that was squarely attributed to Vivienne as one of those "people who just love conflict ... who like to make a mountain out of a molehill, and like to sensationalise. And this is awful to say, but it's true, I'm afraid. There are some people that don't want to have the ultimate objective achieved. There's got to be an obstacle in the way. They've got to be the person that finds the reason why we cannot achieve it, why we cannot do. And that is [Vivienne]."

We can see in this account the social process of "othering" (see Neiterman et al. (2015); Obed Madsen & Vallentin (2018); Baikovich (2020) for discussions of othering in a diversity of work and professional contexts and de Beauvoir (1949) for seminal work on the female Other). By othering, we are referring to processes of stigmatization, which defines another person in a negative manner and compares this "other" in service of one's own positive "alterior" identity. In this case, we see Vivienne vilified as an irrational exaggerator who likes causing trouble and obstructing the progress of the association, in contrast to "good" trustees (like me) who "put their names forward because they want to make a difference ... it might not be a surprise for you to learn that I feel I'm in that latter category." (Chair). In an overtly gendered othering of Vivienne, the CEO began to refer to her in internal conversations with the senior leadership team only as "that woman" and would often refer to the need for board conversations and documentation to pass "the Vivienne test."

Interestingly, I experienced discrepancies in the internal consistency of the Chair's stance towards governance issues in private versus public spaces. While in public, the Chair would back the CEO unequivocally and position any challenge from Vivienne as a show of mistrust. Privately, he shared the perspective of the very trustee he Othered on the matter of CEO–Trustee duality, stating "what would I prefer? Probably for [CEO] to be impartial and objective ... I don't see the benefit of them being a trustee. There's possibly a conflict. I don't see they bring any value as a trustee. I think, if anything, [CEO's] possibly too conflicted."

References

Baikovich, A. (2020). Mobilizing national identity and othering practices as means of resistence. *Organization Science*, https://doi.org/10.1287/orsc.2019.1345.

Bain, C. (2017). *Interplay of Intentions: An Ethnography of Institutional Work Within a Hybrid Organization*. Unpublished DBA (Doctoral) Thesis. Sheffield, UK: Sheffield Hallam University.

de Beauvoir, S. (1949). *The Second Sex*. Alfred: A. Knopf.

DeMaria, W. (2008). Whistleblowers and organizational protesters: Crossing imaginary borders. *Current Sociology*, *56*, 865–883.

Foucault, M. (2001). *Fearless Speech*. Los Angeles, CA: Semiotexte.

Garner, J. T. (2009a). Strategic dissent: Expressions of organizational dissent motivated by influence goals. *International Journal of Strategic Communication*, *3*, 34–51.

Garner, J. T. (2009b). When things go wrong at work: An exploration of organizational dissent messages. *Communication Studies*, *60*(2), 197–218.

Glazer, M., & Glazer, P. (1989). *The Whistleblowers: Exposing Corruption in Government and Industry*. New York, NY: Basic Books.

Goodboy, A. K., Chory, R. M., & Dunleavy, K. N. (2008). Organizational dissent as a function of organizational justice. *Communication Research Reports*, *25*(4), 255–265.

Graham, J. W. (1986). Principled organizational dissent: A theoretical essay. In L. L. Cummings & B. M. Staff (Eds), *Research in Organizational Behavior* (vol. 8, pp. 1–52). Greenwich, CT: JAI Press.

Dick, P., & Coule, T. (2020). Non-compliance with regulatory codes in the nonprofit sector: Accountability and the discursive coupling of means and ends. *Business and Society*, *59*(4), 749–786.

Jos, P., Tompkins, M. E., & Hays, S. W. (1989). In praise of difficult people: A portrait of the committed whistleblower. *Public Administration Review*, *49*, 552–561.

Kassing, J. W. (2000). Exploring the relationship between workplace freedom of speech, organizational identification, and employee dissent. *Communication Research Reports*, *4*, 387–396.

Kassing, J. W. (2008). Consider this: A comparison of factors contributing to employees' expressions of dissent. *Communication Quarterly*, *56*(3), 342–355.

Kassing, J. W. (2009). Articulating, antagonizing, and displacing: A model of employee dissent. *Communication Studies*, *48*(4), 311–332.

King, D., & Griffin, M. (2019). Nonprofits as schools for democracy: The justifications for organizational democracy within nonprofit organizations. *Nonprofit & Voluntary Sector Quarterly*, *48*(5), 910–930.

Mansbach, A. (2009). Keeping democracy vibrant: Whistleblowing as truth-telling in the workplace. *Constellations*, *16*, 363–376.

Miceli, M., & Near, J. (1992). *Blowing the Whistle*. New York, NY: Lexington Books.

Neiterman, E., Salmonsson, L., & Bourgeault, I. L. (2015). Navigating otherness and belonging: A comparative case study of IMG's professional integration in Canada and Sweden. *Ephemera: Theory and Politics in Organization*, *15*(4), 773–795.

Obed Madsen, S., & Vallentin, S. (2018). *The Process of Othering in Public Organisations*. Paper presented at The Academy of Management Annual Meeting 2018. Chicago, United States: Academy of Management.

Orend, B. (2000). *War and International Justice: A Kantian Perspective*. West Waterloo, Ontario: Wilford Laurier University Press.

Rothschild, J. (2013). The fate of whistleblowers in nonprofit organizations. *Nonprofit and Voluntary Sector Quarterly*, *42*(5), 886–901.

8 Leading Away from Purpose and Getting Away with It

> "The CEO 'blew a fuse' and went into what can only be described as a 'screaming fit,' they kept yelling 'the board will have my balls!' – repeatedly"
>
> (Former Director)

Divide and Conquer: Cultivating Fear and Apathy

A plethora of subtle measures emerged within the association that were powerful on a symbolic level in generating fear and apathy among the senior leadership team and beyond. One of the first things the CEO did on moving to their his office, was have the entrance door providing access from the corridor blocked up. This meant that the only way to physically access the CEO was through their Personal Assistant's (PA's) office, and perhaps more importantly, through their actual PA. Concurrently, they were clear in their disdain for email communications (that create an audit trail), particularly on any matter of potential contention as we saw in the previous chapter with regard to the Head of HR.

While the CEO could be very charismatic in their interactions with the board, they took a total disinterest in employees. Though the team in the "Head Quarters" of the association was relatively small, at around 135 staff, the CEO refused to learn anyone's name, beyond the directors as their immediate reports. Even then, their interest was instrumental and based on professional utility. I recall once saying to the CEO that I had to leave early that day to "take Cat to the hospital." Their response was "why are you taking your (pet) cat to a hospital?" I had worked for them for around 8 years at that point, and they had no idea that Cat is short for Catriona, my youngest of two daughters. Such behaviors provide strong cultural cues that you, and social relations in the workplace more generally, are of no (human) value and should be geared only towards profitability (see Fournier & Grey (2000), Grey & Willmott (2005), Adler et al. (2008) for critiques of such approaches to workplace social relations founded upon Critical Management Studies principles).

There were also far less subtle cues regarding human value. In parallel to the arrival of a new CEO, a consultancy company was brought in to "support and mentor him." This seemed to include a review of the whole organization, and the senior leadership team in particular. Alan, a member of the senior leadership team, was not represented favorably in this review, or by some of his director-level colleagues. This reinforced the CEO's rapidly formed judgement that he was "ineffective" in heading up an "underperforming" function. At a team meeting early in the CEO's term of office, it was announced to the directors that Alan had been made aware that there were questions about his ability and that he was required to present to the CEO and senior leadership team at a strategic planning meeting in a few weeks time. Alan's brief for the presentation was to outline an improvement plan for his function, and how he was going to build "better" relationships with the rest of the senior leadership team.

The planning day came, and it was clear that Alan was understandably anxious about his pending presentation. The session itself was just awful. The CEO continually interrupted Alan, vehemently disagreeing with the points he was trying to make and, at one point, began scoffing and laughing at his recommendations. In the moment, I remember thinking that the whole session could have been done in a very different way. That the CEO could have taken a developmental approach with Alan in advance of the presentation, putting him in the best position to be successful in front of his peers. That is what I would have done if this was one of my team members. Instead, I got the impression that the CEO was seeing the presentation for the first time and the session had been set up as some kind of "test," and one that Alan would not pass.

I was incredibly uncomfortable during the presentation; it felt cruel and demeaning and I wanted it to be over as soon as possible. I think others felt the same and rather than engaging with the material, asking questions and debating recommendations productively, there was little comment, minimal questions and no meaningful discussion of the recommendations. The following day, Alan was "let go" with immediate effect. There was no further conversation about Alan or his session at future team meetings. It was almost as if he simply ceased to exist. The only time I heard his name after that was in hushed voices and quiet corners. I took three very clear messages away from this incident. First, the CEO appears to like humiliating people and flexing his power publicly. Second, if you ever have an issue with a team member, do not complain to the CEO or it might result in them, or you, being singled out for the same treatment. Third, always try to be in the CEO's "good books" or, again, you might be singled out for the same treatment. Noel, a former director at the association whose "case" we will discuss later in the chapter noted that Alan "was an easy target to attract the attention of a Bully. He was not liked by [the consultancy company] who acted well and truly as 'Well Poisoners.' [CEO] found Alan too slow and ponderous and Marketing a less than effective business driver – more a useful mouthpiece for the CEO. They did not want a pedestrian manager or function which they did not, in any case, value."

Negative emotional explosions from the CEO involving verbal attacks on individuals, shouting and banging the table with their fists became a norm in monthly senior leadership team meetings. These, to my mind, bullying "results at any cost" behaviors were subsequently reproduced by some other members of the leadership team. As the director with HR in their portfolio, I became aware of several incidents relating to the results of the staff survey, introduced as part of our "Top 100" agenda, outlined in Chapter 4. Two departments' staff satisfaction scores were consistently low, year on year, relative to others in the association. They were accompanied by descriptions of explosive directors who bullied team members, screamed at people and in one case resorted to tears (interpreted as emotional manipulation) in team meetings. On receiving the results of the survey for her department, Mariella convened a team meeting and proceeded to berate her team for producing the lowest scores in the Institute, which made her look bad and could compromise the "Top 100" award. Rather ironically, she reportedly made it very clear that she expected her team to report higher satisfaction in the next survey.

My attempts to deal with the specific instances of alleged bullying highlighted by the survey, and the use of what is supposed to be a developmental process to facilitate organizations in becoming the "best places to work" as a stick to beat people with, were dismissed by the CEO. Their response was that the two directors were only seeking to "motivate" their staff and that it was ok as one of the teams was performing "better than ever." I interpreted this response as the CEO deeming it acceptable, perhaps desirable, for directors to create a culture of fear within their own teams because it led to better results, which in turn may lead to "Top 100" and "Best CEO" accolades for them personally. I was not alone in this type of interpretation, as a former director put it in drawing parallels between the former and incumbent CEOs:

> "In terms of self-efficacy, [former CEO] I think knew themself quite well, albeit they suppressed most emotions. [They] would often avoid difficult decisions relating to people, despite their cold demeanour. When they did make a tough call (as was the case with the Deputy CEO) they agonised over it for some time. [Incumbent CEO] saw these types of choices as brave deeds that should be recognised, admired and lauded. I think they derived significant gratification through the execution of these 'tough decisions.'"

There were ongoing, divisive tactics employed to create disagreement and hostility among members of the senior leadership team. At my annual appraisal with the CEO, for example, there were always two standard questions: 1) what do you think the team are saying to me about you? 2) what do you think about the team? The CEO would then work through the team, one by one. With the experience of Alan etched into my memory, I would always answer the first question with some generalized feedback that I had been given directly from colleagues. We were a small team, so it was easy to have some sense of what people thought of you, though to what degree of honesty was unknown. I refused to answer the second question, saying that I give any feedback I have directly to the individual concerned so there really is no need for me to give it to the CEO. I did not want to be responsible for anyone being singled out because of a comment I made. Nor did I want to be in a position where the CEO had material to report back to my peers, often out of context and almost certainly to create divisions within the team. I often wondered if the CEO provided the impetus for in-fighting among the directors so that we would never unite against them.

The climate within the association had in many ways become toxic. I have colleagues who describe "betrayal" from other directors who "saw advantage" in contributing to their downfall and "some other peers" motivated "by necessity." We have illustrated other instances of questionable behavior towards association members depicted merely as consumers that should be exploited to serve the institute's growth (in Chapter 4) and students on corporate programmes willed to fail in order to generate more revenue (in Chapter 3). My personal experience of most of the individuals involved leads me to believe that they were not inherently "bad people." But faced with a certain set of conditions even "decent people" can make morally dubious decisions and behave poorly. To my mind, Geoff's "keeping me in a job project" represents the verbalization of a fear culture where the focus becomes daily results by any means necessary, because if they are not achieved there is a very real chance you could lose your livelihood. As I hope is evident in the pages of this book, I have my own conscience to wrestle over whether I always went far enough to "do the right thing," or sometimes took the path of least resistance.

Scapegoating and Sacrificial Lambs

In the previous chapter we spent some time discussing the dynamics between Vivienne (the trustee) and the CEO, and the contestation over governance structures, processes and practices. The CEO was experiencing significant "heat" from the board about the appropriateness of organizational governance, pay and reward systems, (purely economic) performance measures and accounting practices in the context of the association as a charity. In particular, Vivienne was "challenging them [CEO] at all the meetings – challenging them at every turn regarding the financial stuff" (Director). Significantly, such challenges had mobilized dissent among other trustees. I recall being present at a board meeting where a trustee asked the CEO to account for some financial matters. In response, the CEO looked over to the Financial Director (FD) for the answer, at which point the trustee said "I didn't ask the FD, I asked the CEO."

Much of the contestation regarding such matters coalesced around or implicated the association's finances, though they were arguably motivated by bigger questions of purpose and the ends to which finances were (or were not) being directed. As the pressure mounted, there was suddenly attention to the similarity in age between the CEO and FD, accompanied by a narrative that it would be "high-risk" and "de-stabilizing" for the holders of these two key positions to retire at the same time. The CEO called the FD to their office and, by the FD's account, casually enquired as to when the FD was thinking of retiring. Not realizing the motivation for the question, he responded with a fairly flippant "oh, in around 2 years my financial situation should be such that I can retire." Not long after, the FD was called back to the CEO's office. The CEO announced, "I have your 2 year package in place; you will remain in the business for 12 months while I recruit a new Chief Operating Officer, then take 6 months garden leave followed by 6 months payment in lieu of notice." My, and the FD's reading was that "someone's head needed to roll" in response to the board's concerns and it was not going to be the CEO's. It often seemed as if the CEO cultivated a culture of blame and distrust between the trustee board and leadership team and there were several other examples of what I came to refer to as "sacrificial lamb" situations. These resulted in termination of employment for senior staff accompanied by significant "compensation" packages. The one that almost broke me, professionally and personally, related to Noel, and occurred not long before the FD's "retirement deal."

My very first memory of Noel extends back to when he applied for his role during the former CEO's term of office. The director-level role that he applied for was one that merged two existing teams, one of which I worked in as a middle manager. These teams were previously managed by separate directors. As a result of a re-structure those directors were made redundant from their role and redeployed to lower-level posts. One reported to Noel and the other to the CEO. Noel stood out in the recruitment process. He was the first "new" director at the association for a long time and the whole process was being watched closely by staff. As soon as the applications came in, we went through them to see if any applicants were already associational members (none was) or had applied for a membership pack. Noel was the only one who had phoned to request a pack in order to do his homework, though he never mentioned this during the selection process. My recollection of him on interview day when, like the other candidates, he was taken on a tour of the different teams and offices was that he was dressed in an obviously expensive but not "showy" suit. He had an incredibly friendly face and took time to speak with and listen to people. Interestingly, I do not remember anything of the other candidates.

When Noel first started at the association, I reported directly to him. I always experienced him as what I would call values-driven. Although he had been Commercial Director in his previous role it was for a major household charity and, at the association, he never presented the need to make money as superseding Charter objects. He often spoke of his first job in a family-owned company that manufactured and sold shoes, and which seemed to have profoundly influenced his view of work organizations. It was owned by a Quaker family and some 30 years later he still spoke about the founding values of the company – equality, peace, truth, justice, simplicity.

Noel had a great capacity to engage people and valued celebration; he always gave each member of staff a card and chocolates for their birthday and would take time to get to know them as people. He often resorted to storytelling to get his points across, rather than "telling" people what to do. He had multifaceted relationships across the world. People were drawn to him by his charisma, his sense of fun and his knowledge of the profession, of learning, of culture, of travel, and of many other bizarre and obscure things. His contact book (then "rolodex") was one of the largest I have seen – in fact there were 2 – and he always knew "someone who can." He could be frustrating too; his pace was at times relentless and his standards were always high.

What he had was of a strong "moral compass" and he used this to guide decision-making. He respected the need to make money and was competitive in his own way about managing the department that was, at that time, the financial engine of the association. That said, like the former CEO, money was not the end game for Noel, and he was always keen to understand what any revenue would be used for. He frequently championed access to learning for disadvantaged groups on the basis that it should enable individuals to gain jobs that provided realistic wages. It was Noel who successfully made the case for members of the profession in a developing country (and former British colony) with significant financial hardships in the early 2000s to receive associational membership and exams free of charge. Without this initiative, professional certification would have been beyond the reach of many citizens of that nation; it was seen as "the right thing to do."

Noel's relationship with the incumbent CEO was changeable and increasingly volatile. Interestingly, it had been Noel who first socialized the CEO into the association, providing introductions to senior professionals and members of the board. In the end, I think he felt somewhat responsible for bringing the CEO into the organization. In the early days, the CEO maintained a close and friendly relationship with Noel, relying on him to "teach him the ways" of the institute. This began to change as the CEO brought in his own people, including those he had worked with in the past. Though their semi-personal friendship started to wane, I always got a sense that the CEO continued to value Noel for his ability to engage people and to develop international opportunities – a trait that was instrumental to the CEO's global ambitions. Noel himself reflected:

> "In my case I was useful to [the CEO] in his early days due to my connections, relationships and general knowledge of the business. This changed rapidly as he became more secure and settled in the organization.
>
> I have to say, leaving the association was both a sad event and a respite experience. The last two years of working with [the CEO] were for me very unhappy ones, in contrast to the previous twelve or so which were exciting, stimulating and highly interesting. It was a real relief to go, but I felt a sadness and guilt toward a lot of good people I had left behind to the whims of the Tyrant King!
>
> The atmosphere that prevailed reminded me of that of a book I had read on the Chinese cultural revolution in 1966–76! If I ever needed an example of a malignant dictatorship, this was it. I did feel remorseful for not fighting for the ones left behind, instead I chose to take the money and run and although beneficial for me, I did not feel good about this."

This sentiment confirmed my belief that the CEO's greed, arrogance and continual demands for "more" put the biggest strain on their relationship. The CEO first put Noel into the Middle East to develop a new hub, and he did this very successfully. From here, Noel was sent to another country to turn around a failing subsidiary. Noel continually challenged the CEO's positioning of this international office as a significant revenue stream for the association and a segue into domination of the region. Yet the CEO continued to present an ambitious turnaround plan to the Board of Trustees. I sat in on monthly meetings between the CEO and FD in the U.K. and Noel and his finance manager overseas. I hated these meetings. The tone was always aggressive and most ended with the CEO shouting at the overseas team, as captured in my field-note diary:

> "The pattern went … the overseas finance manager and U.K. FD would present the numbers and forecast … the CEO would challenge these, Noel would provide reasons why the CEO's numbers were not achievable – for instance, locked in operational costs such as the office that were simply too high, the market not being as mature as the CEO thought, over reliance on one particular

> activity (the conference). The CEO would begin raising their voice, using phrases like 'I want,' 'You are not understanding me,' 'Do I make myself clear.' When really pushed, Noel would intellectualise or tell the CEO why he was wrong, and this always resulted in more yelling. The minutes only ever recorded the financial targets, the forecast (which showed a deficit on targets), and the CEO's demands that the targets were met – never Noel's counter position and his explanations for why the targets were simply unrealistic and unachievable."

These meetings went on for perhaps 6 months, until the conference at the end of the financial year. This was when Noel's forecast of a deficit became a reality and the CEO had to manage the messaging to the board. Because the CEO had failed to accept Noel's repeated early warnings and communicate to the board that progress was slower than planned and why, the trustees reacted badly. They felt the situation had either been deliberately mis-represented to them by the CEO and/or Noel, or that they were incompetent in their role. At the time this incident came to a head, Noel was preparing for stage 2 of the turnaround plan, which had seen him recruit an Operational Manager in the international office and prepare to open an office in another country in the region. My team had been supporting Noel with his re-location and I was aware that all his personal belongings had been packed up and were in transit to his next destination. He was living in a managed apartment for the remaining few weeks.

I was left shaken after being called into the CEO's office to talk about a "change of plans" that ultimately resulted in Noel being "let go." Again, internal communications were carefully managed, and this was officially positioned as a re-alignment and re-prioritization of the association's strategy for that region of the world. I was not convinced of this. The sudden change of plans, the timing of it being the end of the financial year, and the board's recent and strong reaction to the end of year results made it feel more like the CEO wanted to be seen to act and Noel was a convenient scapegoat. Noel provides the following recollection of events in the lead up to this "parting of the ways":

> "The first point to make here was that in some ways I was responsible in an indirect and unconscious way for orchestrating my own departure. After the success in the Middle East, [CEO] looked for me to come up with a solution to the [failing international subsidiary] problem. I told [CEO] it was my belief that the MD (Managing Director) was using the operation almost as his personal "train set" and was ignoring corporate plans, protocols and policies. He was in effect a "Wild Card" and needed to be closely managed and directed. Ever the loyal corporate citizen, I suggested that I went there to conduct a review

of the business and thereafter furnish [CEO] with a report that provided recommendations on the way forward.

Cutting a very long story short my conclusions were that [the international office] was a 'Forlorn Hope' and we should close it down and cut our losses. Unfortunately, accumulated losses over the first five years of the operation had resulted in a debt of just over £800K. The total close down of [the office] was estimated at £950K which would be subject to write off by the association.

I remember [CEO] asking me how long it would take to clear the losses and establish a situation of sustained profitability. I told them I doubted it was possible without major downsizing and restructuring i.e. relocation of office, staff reductions, reduced overheads, focus on correct product mix for the environment etc. My best estimate was that it would take 6 years. The CEO 'blew a fuse' and went into what can only be described as a 'screaming fit', they kept yelling 'the board will have my balls!' Repeatedly!

They asked if I would do my best to straighten the mess out and said that if I could not do it then no one could – false complement but nice! It was decided that [the MD of the international office] would have to go, not least as he had lied to the board about the year's result, banking on receiving a tax refund which did not materialize in the end. The rest you are aware of – my subsequent appointment as a turnaround manager. I took over in the October and the next twelve months were the strangest of my career. In a nutshell the following happened:

- I met with [CEO] in early Jan [15 months after taking over] where they told me I was doing a fantastic job and that they had every confidence I would return a profit of £220K that year. I told them this was completely unrealistic but if we had a decent conference we might break even. They did not want to listen and said they believed their role was the role of a top football manager; to use me as their star striker, to bring me on in the game when we were losing and change things by scoring winning goals!
- We met again in May and again they praised all I was doing and asked me to think of what I wanted to do next – after we had got the international office right this year – and did I want to focus on the development of Academies (none had been developed since I left the Commercial Director Post). Alternatively, they wanted to develop an office in the USA – would I want to do this? All a bit surreal given the train wreck I was driving!
- In July, I attended a SLT (Senior Leadership Team) meeting and it was clear that things had changed; the Sales Director had

convinced the CEO that Academies were just big accounts and not multifaceted one stop shops. The meeting ended in a shouting match and the climate towards me had cooled and I did not know why. I since learned the Sales Director, and two other Directors, were all looking to get involved in parts of the business I was involved in – and had been less than good advocates for me.

- In early November I was sent to [another country in the region] to look for accommodation and take over the operation. I was recalled in December to the UK and Carole, the rest is now ancient history!

The above sequence presented a very mixed message to me, which left me perplexed and confused. As late as October, [CEO] still seemed to want to talk about what challenges lay ahead for me in relation to the USA. I realized that the three other Directors I have mentioned had ambitions in my remit and they took full advantage when it was clear that I was falling out of favor. For my part I do not blame anyone for their behaviors during this time – it was an extremely volatile, dangerous and unstable situation with [CEO] appearing to change their mind on a continuous basis. This situation created an 'everyone for themselves' environment of survivability.

I am quite clear what the drivers were that fuelled my departure of which there were three:

1 The CEO needed a scapegoat to blame for the failure to deliver their promise of a turnaround in one year to an ill-informed and less than competent board.
2 In the convoluted mind of [the CEO], they also wanted someone they could punish on the grounds that they had let [the CEO] down and as such caused their judgement to be suspect in their own eyes and in their masters'.
3 In practical terms I was expensive and getting shot of me realised a substantive saving which they could present as a bonus and good management housekeeping applied to a bad set of circumstances."

By removing Noel from the association, the CEO arguably distracted the board from their personal actions and culpability by signaling that the "poor performance" was a result of Noel's (in)capability. In contrast, I always felt that it was down to an ill-informed, unrealistic strategy, an impatience to get things done and a lack of investment, which meant the small team in the international office could not work at speed. That particular office did eventually reach a marginal surplus but never achieved the projected surplus in the intervening 5 years, for the exact reasons Noel consistently outlined to the CEO in those unbearable meetings.

As was often the case with senior level "exits" from the association, it fell on me to manage the process. This was without question one of the most painful experiences of my life and I struggled intensely with what I felt was a cruel and unjust process. Although I never felt Noel needed my protection, I felt incredibly protective of him and deeply worried about the potential impact on his health and well-being. My first act was to call Noel and ask him to return to the U.K. instead of his next overseas assignment. In all honesty, I cannot recall what I said on that call, but Noel has told me since that I had worked hard to signal what was to come without actually saying it. This enabled him to prepare as far as one ever can for such an event.

The situation got worse when, before Noel arrived back in the U.K., the CEO instructed me to find a way to break the severance aspect of Noel's employment contract, as it was too costly. I was incensed. It demonstrated a lack of integrity and honesty. Noel had not been incompetent or derelict of his duties so there was no misconduct or poor-performance case. The CEO had not been under duress when they originally signed that contract; they had now simply changed their mind. It demonstrated a total lack of personal responsibility. In my view, it was the CEO's unwillingness to accept and communicate Noel's forecasts and recommendations to the board that resulted in them feeling "stage-managed" and misled. It demonstrated an absence of loyalty to a colleague who had achieved many successes and played an instrumental part in growing the association. It demonstrated a worrying lack of humanity. Noel was essentially fired 4 days before Christmas, leaving him jobless, homeless and possession-less as his new home – due to his work for the association – was almost 7,000 miles away. The CEO showed no discernible concern for this and it required a legal battle for them to cover the costs of a hotel until Noel was able to find a new home in the U.K. The main emotion I saw from the CEO was exasperation that Noel would not bow down to their demands, which was negatively impacting on *their* Christmas.

I have often reflected on that time and its emotional cost to me. I have described it numerous times as "bringing me to my knees." Some people might say that I was derelict in my professional role and put my personal relationship with Noel first. He has on several occasions expressed gratitude to me for "subtly fighting [his] corner almost as a double agent" and "helping [him] in a covert way, allowing him to prepare for the worst and plan for the best." It is true that I forewarned Noel about what was to come, thus allowing him to prepare. I also worked hard to make sure that the contract was honored in full. This included bringing in an external legal team to help me explain to the CEO why they could not legally reduce the compensation to Noel. Eventually, when I still could not move the CEO, I asked the Chair of the board to instruct them to honor the contract because it was the right and legal thing to do. I do not, however, feel in my heart that I was derelict of my duty. As an HR professional, one of my roles is to "protect" the organization. For me, this means protecting its values (not the CEO), ensuring it is a viable and valued place to work, and protecting the association's brand as an employer. At the time I was very emotionally driven to "do the right thing" and this meant making sure we acted legally and with integrity, honesty and fairness to Noel. I wanted the process of Noel's exit from the association to be done "right," even if the overall decision was not "right" in the first place. Over time and on reflection, I take myself back to the term of office of the former CEO, when the association's KPIs were not only about the ends we achieved, but also the means by which we achieved those ends.

Noel seems to have reached a place where he is both philosophical and pragmatic, providing these reflections on the incident:

> "My personal efficacy and strength of character allowed me to see the situation as it really was. So, the feelings of being undervalued, written off, undermined, etc. which are sometimes usual in these cases were not evident to me. I came out of the negotiation period battered, bruised, stressed. Having said all this, this experience happening alongside my marital issues of the time made me reflect very deeply on who I had become up to that point. This also caused me to analyse who I wanted to be in the future and what changes I needed to effect in order to be a better person. It was an important intervention that enabled me to reframe rather than reinvent myself – keeping the existing good (hopefully?), shedding the less attractive and developing and adding new aspects to my spiritual psyche. I would also state that I bear no ill will toward [the CEO]; for me it was not personal and when I now reflect on the matter I feel real sorrow and yes, a level of pity, for the type of person [they] had become."

We have seen, particularly in this and the previous chapter, some of the CEO's tactics to suppress dissidence and distract from personal accountability in order to maintain power, control and authority. I often reflect on what may have led to such tyranny in management; was the CEO consciously modeling their behavior on someone they respected? Were they adopting the military strategies they studied in their history degree? Or, was there something more personal driving such behaviors? I have not reached an answer to this question, and nor is that the purpose of this book. But I remain both fascinated and perplexed as to how quickly such unnecessarily cruel and immoral behavior became pervasive and unchallenged in an organization that was, such a short time ago, driven by values of community, family, moral responsibility and service (to the profession). Scholarship that integrates insights from psychiatry and psychology with management and organization theory reveals much about the underlying causes and patterns of many seemingly intractable problems or "neuroses" (some of which are evident in this book), tracing them from organizational to individual levels (see, for example, Kets de Vries & Miller, 1984; Babiak & Hare, 2007; 2019).

References

Adler, P. S., Forbes, L. C., & Willmott, H. (2008). Critical management studies. *The Academy of Management Annals*, *1*, 119–179.

Babiak, P., & Hare, R. D. (2007). *Snakes in Suits: When Psychopaths Go to Work*. New York: Harper Collins.

Babiak, P., & Hare, R. D. (2019). *Snakes in Suits: Understanding and Surviving the Psychopaths in Your Office*. New York: Harper Collins.

Fournier, V., & Grey, C. (2000). At the critical moment: Conditions and prospects for critical management studies. *Human Relations*, *53*(1), 7–32.

Grey, C. & Willmott, H. C. (Eds.) (2005). *Critical Management Studies: A Reader*. Oxford, UK: Oxford University Press.

Kets de Vries, M. F. R., & Miller, D. (1984). *The Neurotic Organization: Diagnosing and Changing Counterproductive Styles of Management*. San Francisco, CA: Wiley Jossey-Bass.

9 Conclusion

We have concerned ourselves in this book with the nature of managerial work in nonprofit organizations generally and that work which is dedicated to organizational transformation specifically. Some readers may have felt surprise, disbelief, frustration, anger, disappointment and many other emotions at some of the organizational and individual behaviors that occurred within the association. We (re)experienced all of this while writing our story of the organization, despite its familiarity as a research endeavor and lived experience. Recent media coverage of charity scandals involving sexual abuse, fraud, unfair treatment of whistleblowers, payment of trustees and other wrongdoings further underlines that immoral behavior is not simply the monopoly of the corporate sector nor is civic virtue a given in nonprofit organizations. The virtues often assigned to nonprofits by policymakers, academics and wider society – democracy, social justice, equity to name but a few – are not inherent qualities but interactional accomplishments that require institutional work by those who govern, work and volunteer within social purpose organizations.

Returning to the questions with which we opened our introductory chapter, our insider account of just one organization illustrates that space has and can be opened up for the wholesale importation of managerialism into the nonprofit sphere, and that nonprofits can indeed be at risk of reconstitution as primarily economic entities, serving the interests of a leadership elite. We have also narrated the implications of this for the nature of organizing – structurally, politically, symbolically and rhetorically – for particular groups (e.g. trustees, staff, associational members) and for the dynamics of contestation. Strikingly, our account shows that such ideological transformations not only can and do happen, but that they are possible within organizations characterized by a long history, long-term inhabitants and a deeply embedded social purpose script – and within a relatively short time span.

The ideologies and practices associated with this transformation deviate from widely accepted social norms and expectations of this category or type of organization. Yet, for proponents of the classical view of the firm, and in an institutional context that blurs the boundaries between corporate, public and nonprofit organizing, such ideological cross-overs will likely become more commonplace and normalized. From a corporate organizing logic, the actions of the association's incumbent CEO, whose professional socialization occurred entirely in the corporate world, would not be considered particularly unusual. In fact, the structures they instituted are commonly purported to assist CEOs in attaining superior performance through exercising "complete authority over the corporation [so] their role is unambiguous and unchallenged" and so that "the organization will enjoy the classic benefits of unity of direction and of strong command and control" (Donaldson & Davis, 1991, pp. 51–52).

The normative theory of business ethics advanced by thinkers such as Milton Friedman holds that the firm has no social responsibility to the public or society. In fact, he argues that:

> "Few trends could so thoroughly undermine the very foundations of our free society as the acceptance by our corporate officials of a social responsibility other than to make as much money for their stockholders as possible."
>
> (Friedman, 1970)

According to Friedman, the only responsibility of the corporate firm is to increase profits through activities that stay within the rules of the game (open and free competition without deception or fraud). He argued that executives spending money on social causes were spending someone else's money for their own purposes. Of course, this classical shareholder doctrine is controversial among (often left-wing) contemporary thinkers who claim it is financially, economically, legally, socially and morally wrong. That it impoverishes citizens and enriches corporate elites (see, for example, Duska 1997; 2007; Klein, 2007). At the heart of this alternative approach is the idea that all organizations (including corporations) must take into consideration society's views on what constitutes a legitimate exercise of power on the premise that directors cannot govern organizations in opposition to the values of the society in which they are embedded (Gomez & Korine, 2008). It seems to us that the "war" in the association started with the (re)negotiation of organizational means and ends. The former CEO was, as many have said, as commercially savvy as the next, but money was always a means to an end. It was oxygen to enable the association to serve its profession and this higher purpose permeated the cultural fabric of the association. It was when the relentless pursuit of profit maximization and growthism, arguably at the cost of humanity towards the association's inhabitants, members and wider profession, was reconstituted as the end game itself that the unrest began.

In the context of "charity," ownership is neither legally possible or desirable; unpaid trustees act as stewards of the organization's assets and are required to direct resources towards public good. Thus, the opposite of Friedman's arguments about executives holds "true" – executives spending money on *anything other than* social causes are spending someone else's money for their own purposes. Indeed, a fellow director once said to me, "the problem with [incumbent CEO] is that they want to run this place, and benefit from the financial returns, like it is their own company, but without taking any risks with their own personal capital." Our point here is that judgments of "right" and "wrong" are contextually sensitive. They are profoundly influenced by individuals' socialization and identification with one organizing logic or another (and its associated systems of belief, ethics and praxis), alongside wider societal norms and expectations of particular types of organization.

In concluding the book, we wish to primarily turn to how such a dramatic change in an organization's trajectory was brought about, drawing together the various strands of institutional work explored across the preceding chapters. We find that two forms of work are central to the logic "war" within the association. First, there is the managerial work undertaken to encourage other organizational inhabitants to identify with senior managers' proffered organizing logic (corporate/community) while maintaining (at least ceremonially) faithfulness to the association's existing mission. We refer to this as *Identification Work*. Second, there is the managerial work undertaken to promote widespread adoption of practices that are congruent with those logics among organizational inhabitants. We term this *Practice Work*. This work is undertaken over time, is mutually reinforcing and often overlapping. The forms of work and their interrelationships are illustrated in Figure 9.1 and then unpacked throughout this chapter.

Identification Work and Hybrid Organizing

Identification work takes place at an ideological level and aims to ensure widespread acceptance of a system of ideas and ideals within the prevailing mission of the organization, but which may nevertheless appear contradictory or illegitimate to its inhabitants. As such, its intent is different from Gawer & Phillip's (2013) notion of "identity work" that sets out to change perceptions of the organization's identity from one "type" of organization to another. Accounts of institutional work that attempt to shift organizations and their inhabitants from one prevailing identity or purpose to another are relatively commonplace within the literature (see Coburn, 2004; Lawrence & Suddaby, 2006; Powell & Colyvas, 2008; Battilana & Dorado, 2010; Turco, 2012; Gawer & Phillips, 2013).

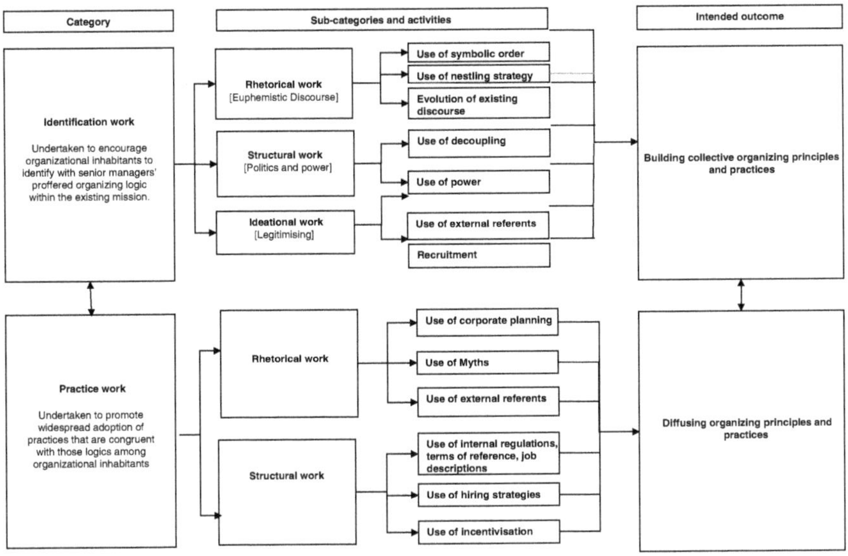

Figure 9.1 Summary of institutional work within the association
Source: Adapted from Bain (2017)

Yet, scant attention has been given to the types of work concerned with influencing the acceptance of a new frame of ideas and ideals within a prevailing, long-held mission. We have offered here a rare longitudinal account of the processes used to encourage inhabitants of the association towards ideological allegiance to an alternative (corporate) logic, and subsequently think and behave in ways congruent with that logic within a prevailing yet inherently contradictory public good mission. Specifically, as elite actors in the association aimed to increase its commercial success, they concurrently attempted to convince others to accept a corporate logic as legitimate within the prevailing context of being a public good organization governed by charter status and charity law. This involved three sub-categories of identification work: (1) rhetorical work (2) structural work and (3) ideational work.

Rhetorical Work

We observe in the pages of this book, senior management's development of what Turco (2012) calls a euphemistic discourse in order to persuade others to identify with their proffered logic. Euphemistic discourses are those which use polite indirect expressions to replace messages that may be offensive to their audience. Specifically, the rhetoric "we make money to do more things/further the institute ..." featured in Chapter 2 encourages staff to accept (and identify with) the creation of profit as a legitimate end-goal for the association. It is nevertheless quite a complex process that involves (a) protection of the existing symbolic order to provide an underlying structure of meaning (b) the use of a nestling strategy that enables new ideas to be fitted to prevailing normative scripts thus giving them moral legitimacy and (3) the evolution of an existing discourse to create a "bridging" effect.

Like many in the association, I was inducted into a symbolic order that prioritized public good and a sense of community with an accompanying "we make money to do more public good" rhetoric under the leadership of the former CEO. Within this frame, making money was purposeful but only as "oxygen" for the organization's survival and not as an end in and of itself. The meaning of public good was explicit, linked to Charter objects and coalesced around helping individuals and organizations in the profession, representing the profession and delivering improved methods. As we narrated, a notably abbreviated version of this phrase is still prevalent today "we make money to do more good stuff/to further benefit the institute." Crucially, the statement retains the opening "we make money to do ..." which has a high degree of familiarity and acceptance with longstanding inhabitants of the association, in that money is positioned as a purposeful resource. However, the narrative has reduced the major premise that defines the use the money is put to, namely the achievement of public good as defined by Royal Charter. Today, the end of the strap line either provides an opaque, unspecified notion of "good stuff" or moves the focus to being in service of the institute itself, rather than the profession it exists to advance. By removing the link to the Charter, the purpose for which funds are generated becomes eroded, enabling space for a new "purpose" – maximization of profit – to be developed as a legitimate end game.

Elite actors then capitalized on the space created through the absence of specified "public good" by nestling new ideas, such as profit sharing (see Chapter 6), into the prevailing script. Logically, this would likely be received as offensive, self-serving and illegitimate by those who identify with a public good ethos or community logic. Yet, in a context where "the further benefit of the institute" has become a legitimized end goal due to its assumed "downstream" contribution to public good, profit sharing became naturalized and uncontroversial to all but a minority. Indeed, it was presented as a moral imperative when the incumbent CEO remarked, "it is fundamentally wrong for the organisation to be making significant profits and not distributing some of this back to staff."

The vagueness of exactly what constitutes "more stuff," "good use" or "furthering the institute" also allows for the creation of a bridging narrative that is suggested to promote logic combination (Battilana &

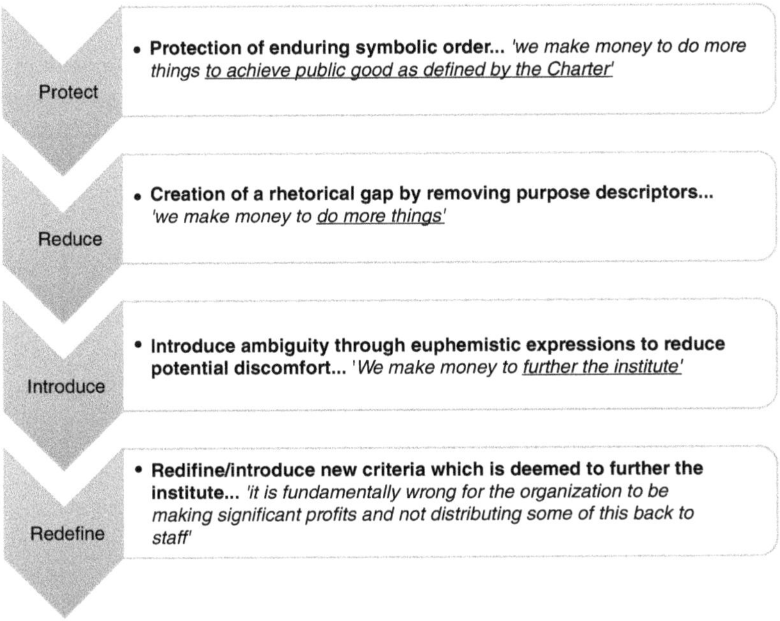

Figure 9.2 Processes of rhetorical transformation within identification work
Source: Bain (2017)

Dorado, 2010). The purpose of a bridging narrative is to strike a balance with the intention of preventing subgroups and schisms coalescing around the competing logics within the organization. This enables organizational action (Green et al., 2009) as inhabitants identifying with divergent corporate and community organizing principles can imbue the message with cognitive meaning for themselves, as we saw in the multiple framings of the association in Chapter 2.

Let's also not forget an important contextual feature that provided supporting architecture for this rhetorical work: a "disastrous" appointment of a CEO from a nonprofit, professional association background who was removed by the board of trustees after only a short time due to poor financial management. This provided the soon-to-be-incumbent CEO, then on the board of trustees, with a moment to create a "burning platform" around the financial state of the association and present commerciality and becoming big business-like as the logical solution. It is interesting that the trustee, Vivienne, and senior manager, Mariella, utilized the same approach of catastrophizing to create a sense of regulatory-related danger in contesting this commercial ideology (see Chapters 3 and 7). Figure 9.2 depicts the process of rhetorical transformation underpinning identification work.

Structural Work

Structural work is the second form of identification work. It refers to work undertaken to re-structure the organization (e.g. its committees, governance, subsidiaries) to align to a particular logic. Such structural work is nevertheless ideological as its purpose is to generate widespread acceptance of a system of (structural) ideas and ideals, which might normatively appear contradictory or illegitimate within the prevailing mission of the association.

By way of illustration, we narrated in Chapter 5 the decoupling of "charity" from "everyday business." Decoupling is a structural process through which an organization takes on several distinct forms and in doing so projects legitimacy to stakeholders (Pache & Santos, 2010, p. 972). The creation of a subsidiary charity with separate branding, financial systems and governance system to which the association – also a registered charity – would annually donate a percentage of its "profits" was technically and legally unnecessary. Symbolically, however, it is a powerful means to separate out, or decouple, "charity" and notions of public good from "core business"; positioning it as an activity rather than the core being of the organization. This move seemed to achieve two things.

First, charity is narrated as being "a small part of what we do" and not something we are, relegating the previously dominant community logic and its organizing principles to a subservient position. This – alongside other change efforts – created space for some senior managers to corral the association towards economic goals as an end in themselves to the point that others internalized those goals and began exploiting themselves, associational members and clients, and socially disciplining peers in the name of economic performance and being "great" employees (see Chapter 4). Such conformism, particularly when encouraged by direct management action to quash dissent and create a culture of fear (see Chapters 7 and 8), suppresses democratic dialogue about the legitimacy and appropriateness of particular goals and values, further bolstering established class and authority structures (see Chapters 5 and 6).

Second, the annual donation of money to the Foundation became a mechanism to legitimate commercial activity and counter any claims from internal constituents that the association was "too commercial." It lent itself to the opaque notion of doing "good stuff" discussed earlier, on the basis that the commercial behaviors within the parent charity (now "the business") were a justified course of action in order to deliver a large donation to the subsidiary charity to do public good. This is a classic model for corporate philanthropy.

That is not to say that the material (financial) and symbolic (cultural and identity) benefits stemming from charity status are not valued by the business, but that their value rests in utilizing this status for economic gain. For example, "tax exemption benefits" are readily acknowledged, as is the ability to differentiate the organization from "charlatans" and other "cheque-book (money orientated) institutions." In this sense, the association's legal status as a charity is used as a Trojan Horse (Pache & Santos, 2013), selectively and episodically coupled with corporate activity to differentiate it from and give it higher moral status when competing with overtly commercial organizations. This creates something of an ideological paradox insofar as elite actors who identify with a corporate logic simultaneously use structure to side-line the organization's social purpose, while utilizing it to gain moral legitimacy with specific audiences for the purposes of competitive advantage.

There were also instances of structures being used as a power resource, so that individual or groups of elite actors could maintain their dominance or challenge that of others. We saw the transformation of governance structures, processes and practices instigated by the CEO that aimed to reduce the formal powers and influence of the association's members, remove processes and reduce the number of groups able to hold the CEO to account or control their use of resources for example. At the same time, the CEO sought to increase their own powerbase through CEO–Trustee duality and informally influencing selection of the Chair of the board (see Chapter 5). The Chair, in a "quid pro quo" arrangement, would then unilaterally approve the CEO's proposals in the event they came under fire from the wider trustee group that, under charity law, are required to act collectively. We suggest these actions were ideologically driven based on a corporate logic where ultimate authority rests with "top management." The Board of Trustees, in challenges often led by Vivienne, countered this move by (re)asserting their control through the introduction of a new audit sub-committee and requests for full governance reviews, including the legality of committee structures/powers and the CEO–Trustee's right to vote (see Chapter 7). As an expert in charity governance in her own right, Vivienne successfully mobilized other members of the board to question the appropriateness of decisions and actions in the name of "good governance" and within the specific ideal of the association as a charity. This, at least to a degree, stifled the absolute authority of the CEO and their proffered corporate organizing principles.

Ideational Work

Ideational work is the third and final form of identification work we observed. It refers to work aimed towards the creation of alternative ways of thinking by specifying abstract categories and elaborating chains of cause and effect (see Lawrence & Suddaby, 2006; Currie et al., 2012). Creating alternative ideals that reflect a given logic is not enough (Gawer & Phillips, 2013), organizational inhabitants must be convinced that the new ideal is appropriate or legitimate; this is the role of ideational work. It seemed to us that several areas of work served this end, including the CEO's selection of employees and trustees in their own image – often referred to in the recruitment world as affinity bias – and the co-optation of external experts.

Throughout this book we have accounted for the presence of the incumbent CEO's "completely different ideology" to his predecessor alongside the implications this had for how the association was structured and work was organized in pursuit of "a whole lot more professionalism." Changes to the governance system privileged "big businesspeople" as a "better" type of people – more rounded, more business-like, more professional, more like the CEO. The argument was that this would facilitate organizational growth and reduce the dysfunction and amateurism caused by the existing representational group, drawn from the profession the association exists to serve (see Chapter 6). From this theorization, the CEO was able to create alternative ways of thinking that resulted in the new "ideal" of being "more like a conventional business." By surrounding themself with individuals who brought to the decision-making process similar interpretations, frames of reference, and experiences, the CEO looked to reduce challenges, reduce the likelihood of disparate ideological coalitions or schisms forming and signal to other actors that a corporate logic was legitimate within the prevailing social mission of the association.

We also saw the co-optation of external experts to legitimate the CEO's desired path to a "more professional," streamlined board composed of "big business people" (see Chapter 5). Well-respected, independent experts served as an influential mechanism both to support the need for dramatic changes to prevailing governance norms at this ideological level, and to defend prevailing practices within the logic war, as we will explore later under rhetorical practice work. What this points to, is the overlapping, mutually reinforcing nature of identification work (at the ideological level) and practice work (at the level of policies, procedures and processes). It also brings our attention to organizational change as a dynamic and rather messy phenomenon. Rather than a single linear process shifting from one steady state (or logic) to another, transformation of the ideological foundations of the association was underpinned by many sites or events of contestation occurring in tandem and creating arenas of contradiction in the underpinning ideals of the organization. It seems to us that it is the interplay of these microdynamics that has significant implications for the practice and theorization of change within hybrid organizations. For example, Vivienne (and to a lesser extent Mariella) presenting the ideals of public good as the organization's reason for being is in dynamic tension with the CEO's presentation of the material and symbolic benefits that being a charity brings to commercial endeavors. This resulted in interruptions to

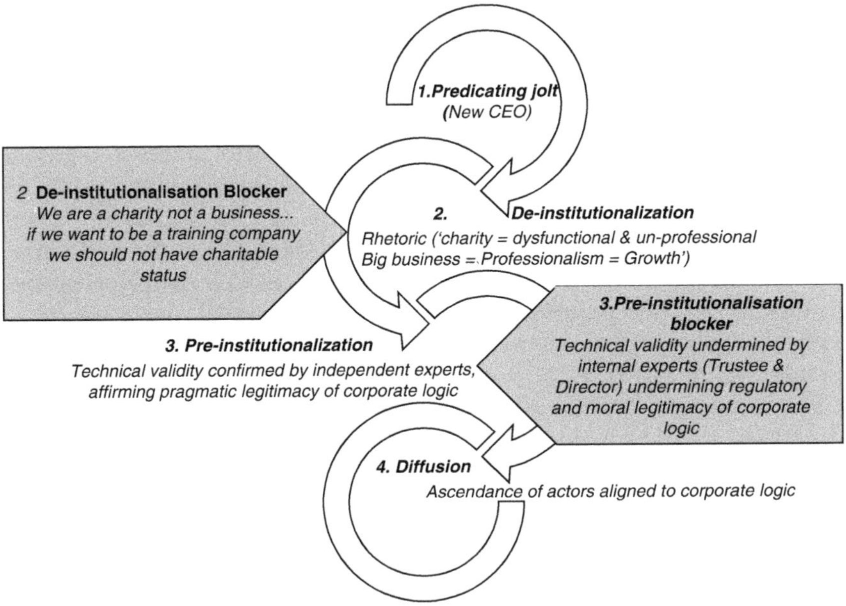

Figure 9.3 Processes of ideational transformation within identification work
Source: Bain (2017)

discourses, of organizing principles and control of work, making decision-making inefficient and often war-like as opposing coalitions formed based on alignment to community or corporate logics (see Figure 9.3 for a depiction of the processes of ideational change).

Practice Work and Hybrid Organizing

Accompanying this work at the ideological level was the managerial work directed towards promoting adoption of practices and behaviors congruent with specific logics among organizational inhabitants. This work takes place at the level of policies, procedures, processes and systems and aims to diffuse a system of collective ideas and ideals through rule setting, monitoring and sanctioning. To put it another way, it is the work undertaken to develop, implement and encourage adoption of practices that reinforce the proffered logic as useful, meaningful and legitimate (Gawer & Phillips, 2013). Specifically, within the context of this book, it relates to managerial efforts both to align practices to the new, emerging corporate logic and to defend and retain practices aligned to the institutionalized community logic. The categories of practice work parallel categories of identification work in that they relate to rhetorical and structural aspects of organizing, but they differ in purpose.

Rhetorical Practice Work

We have seen throughout the pages of this book the managerial time and effort spent, through spoken and written word, introducing and ensuring adoption of new commercial practices. In particular, Chapter 4 narrated the evolution of corporate planning, based on the tactics and language of military strategy, which reconstituted economic performance and global growth as the criteria on which the success of the association and its employees should be judged. The institution of new quarterly "town hall" meetings to report on progress against these objectives and circulation of monthly financial reports to all staff provided rhetorical spaces to diffuse concrete practices that disciplined individual and team behaviors towards profit maximization as a useful, unchallenged end in itself. In addition to this type of "positive" incentivization, there were also the CEO sponsored "corrective" activities such as high-profile taskforces developed to address poor (financial) performance – the "keep me in a job project" and "project eagle" discussed in Chapters 3 and 4 respectively are examples – or the scapegoating of senior managers (see Noel's case in Chapter 8).

That is not to say that corporate rhetoric and practices went completely unchallenged. A notable example of defending against the evils of overly commercial behavior within the association was the interplay, or perhaps "powerplay," between the two directors in Chapter 3. In this scenario, the "protector of public good" rhetorically positioned themselves – and their team – as the moral authority. They were unique to all directors as they were the "only one with a public good mandate" and as such the only one with such a "terrifying" and difficult role. They made use of external referents (consultants and independent regulatory experts) to reinforce and legitimate their expert authority, implementing training to reinforce the technical competency of the team, and director, responsible for regulatory audit and the practices they prescribe. Finally, they catastrophized personal consequences should a breach of regulation (and the "proper" prescribed practices) occur through perpetuating the myth that they would go to prison. As we saw in Chapter 3, this myth acted as a powerful discursive resource to counterbalance, disrupt, dismiss and ridicule commercially driven practices as inappropriate, lacking in integrity and damaging to public good.

Concurrently, and facing normative pressure to conform to the CEO's demands for growth in revenue, Geoff (the other director-level protagonist in the Chapter 3 incident) rhetorically positioned the practices prescribed by the protector of public good as a hinderance to "moneymaking." He positioned them as creating a poor business model that meant "we end up portraying a fairly fragmented image of what our total capability is because there are bits of it that we can only talk to a certain audience about and there are other bits that we clearly can't talk to any part of the student audience about." Geoff also created a powerful narrative of personal risk to his job should commercial objectives not be met (the "keeping me in a job project") that compelled members of the taskforce and his wider team towards money-making at any cost in order to "save" their director.

In other examples of contestation, contradictions between an espoused theory for change and proposed, associated new practices were mobilized to challenge seemingly incongruent messages. The incident between the Head of HR and CEO involved the CEO advocating an "ethos of sharing success" as the justificatory basis for changes to the bonus scheme, while designing a scheme that would, in practice, reward the leadership class disproportionately more than everyone else. Concerned that, rather than sharing success, the proposed scheme would in fact create (or rather deepen) "a culture of elitism," the Head of HR exposed and mounted a challenge to this contradiction. In several arenas we see multiple actors – the head of HR and the director, Mariella – turn rhetoric against logic change, by turning messages regarding the value of new practices in on themselves to expose their violation of the organization's prevailing social mission or their espoused (socially equitable) purposes.

In sum, there was a good deal of rhetorical work to promote the adoption of practices and behaviors congruent with the "we make more money to further the institute" rhetoric and ultimately identification with a corporate organizing logic. Interestingly, it was the rhetorical work at the level of practices, rather than ideology, that was most contested by organizational inhabitants at different levels of the organizational hierarchy. We suggest this may be a result of practices being more "concrete" or less ambiguous in nature than the euphemistic discourse developed through rhetorical identification work, which was sufficiently opaque for inhabitants to imbue it with their own meaning.

Structural Practice Work

The second form of practice work is that undertaken to achieve structural alignment (in teams, jobs, committees) with a specific logic. Examples of structural practice work in this study included: (1) use of governance regulations, terms of reference and job descriptions (2) hiring strategies and (3) incentivization strategies.

Re-aligning governance practices to a corporate logic, where the top executive is autonomous and (in the absence of shareholders) the ultimate authority, involved:

- changes to the association's internal governance regulations to allow CEO–Trustee duality and associated voting rights, shortening the

tenure-ship of trustees and limiting them to one term of office to mitigate challenges from within the board itself;
- attempts to remove the membership body's powers to instigate a vote of no-confidence in the trustee board (which now included the CEO);
- disbanding sub-committees such as that formed solely to monitor and approve executive pay and transferring reformed terms of reference to "new" committees with a broadened remit of financial governance to distract from a singular, contested issue.

In respect of paid employees, and in a similar way to terms of reference at the governance level, the association used job descriptions to define the purpose and structure of specific job roles, their task responsibilities and the basis for making decisions. Unlike the content of governance regulations and terms of reference, which were amended by the company secretary at the behest of the CEO, the authoring process for job descriptions was decentralized to the recruiting director. Although a standard template was provided by the central HR team, directors had a great deal of scope to shape the content of job descriptions within their teams and also author their own evolving job descriptions. As we demonstrated in Chapter 3, in this scenario job descriptions can become an external expression of the organizing logics with which individuals identify and can thus set individual managers, functions and departments against each other based on allegiance to one set of principles and practices or another.

The theorization of "businesspeople" as a better kind of person to take the association forward discussed under ideational work earlier was accompanied by changes in hiring strategies to select both trustees and employees. Governance structures and practices were evolved to reduce member representation, elected by the wider membership body, and prioritize primarily people with corporate experience, by a committee selection process. As we saw in Chapter 5, this selection committee was heavily, but unofficially, influenced by the CEO via "the long list, the short list and the secret list." In a similar fashion, the recruitment practices for employees was re-oriented to attract and build a corpus of people with corporate backgrounds. Advertisement mechanisms moved away from the association's own Website and specialist nonprofit recruitment agencies to new recruitment agencies with more of a commercial focus. High power distance pay and reward systems were redesigned to enhance the remuneration packages of the leadership class. Management roles were restructured to introduce a new tier of "middle managers" and reshape director-level (senior management) roles towards growth and profit generation. Increased delivery to corporates and reformulating knowledge as a commodity to be marketed and sold to consumers were key mechanisms to achieve these economic goals.

New directors were then recruited to sales, marketing and corporate delivery roles; all were exclusively socialized in large, corporate firms.

Incentivization strategies were central to wider socialization of long-serving and new inhabitants with corporate organizing principles and practices. Changes to the bonus scheme, from a modest collective thank you based on means *and* ends criteria to a high-value, multifaceted pay and reward system triggered solely by financial performance incentivized individualistic behavior and diffused a "maximum profit through any means necessary" mentality throughout the association (see Chapter 6). Signaling the primacy of revenue generation through providing a higher total reward opportunity for those occupying sales roles and through notions of what it means to be a "great" employee are all powerful disciplining structures for driving individual and collective decision-making and action towards financial ends.

In sum, the multiple, interlocking messages signaled by changes to material practices in governance, hiring and incentivization, for example, represent persuasive arguments for the adoption and diffusion of particular logics. More broadly, our examination of institutional work at the ideological and practice level highlight the dynamic complexity, interconnectedness and temporal nature of the different forms of work undertaken to maintain (or defend) and transform organizing logics, alongside some of the motivations for doing so. Such work is inter-related, mutually reinforcing, often overlapping, inefficient and messy, and often undertaken in a conflicted, war-like environment. Bringing about change in hybrid organizations is chaotic, often highly contested and involves acts of power, persuasion and authority. In our understanding, there is often no big, bold act but rather an edging process over time that uses subtle and apparently benign changes that eventually break down previous boundaries and create new frameworks of meaning, sensemaking and praxis. This can mitigate the risks of insiders identifying changes as illegitimate in the first place, as well as allowing the instigator to test and respond to the reactions of others if they are detected and perceived negatively. It also holds significant implications for how we study, understand and practice organizational change, insofar as understanding the complexity of such work is a long-term endeavor, involving significant time in the "waiting room" (Mannay & Morgan, 2015) and requiring observation of the actual micro-processes of organizing and managing work over time. Retrospective accounts collected at a single point in time are likely inadequate for developing rich understandings of the role of everyday talk and action in hybrid organizations or the practicalities of change efforts. We agree that this is best served by "dirty," "messy" ethnographic writing that is not "totally repressed by logic, rationality, linearity and coherence" (Pullen & Rhodes, 2008, p. 242; see also Höpfl, 2007; Ericsson & Kostera, 2020).

Concluding Remarks

Many nonprofit scholars have appropriated the fashionable hybridity concept to account for both the entrepreneurial turn in many traditional charities and the upsurge in social enterprises and social entrepreneurship more broadly. There is no doubt that most nonprofits today can meet the criteria to be defined as such. They are *subject to multiple regulatory regimes* through general regulators based on (often multiple) legal status (e.g. the U.K. Charity Commission and Companies House) and according to their field of work (ofqual for education charities or the Care Quality Commission for health and social care providers and so on). They are *embedded within multiple normative orders* (i.e. standards or rules that specify what particular types of organization should do, be or look like), where the boundaries among state, voluntary and corporate action have become blurred and increasingly fluid over time. Finally, they are *constituted by more than one cultural logic,* simultaneously needing to be business-like to generate revenue within an increasingly marketized world (commercial enterprises), while acting as purveyors of social goods (moral enterprises). But, if all nonprofits are constituted as hybrid organizations that can blend and synergize multiple logics in a relatively unproblematic way (Haveman and Rao 2006; Jay, 2013; Skelcher and Smith, 2015), the concept becomes a wasteland of meaning and of little theoretical or practical value. It also positions hybrid organizing as a "win–win," making organizations more financially efficient and socially effective (Mongelli et al., 2019) through (re)organizing work and (re)structuring organizations to better accommodate divergent logics. We have shown, quite starkly, in our account of the association that this "win–win" cannot be taken as a natural given. In fact, it can serve as a powerful discursive resource to justify the (irrational) pursuit of maximum financial returns in organizations that purportedly exist primarily for social purposes.

Theoretically, our ethnographic account adds significant nuance to current theorizations of nonprofit hybridity through sharper attention to the dynamic tensions between logics that undergird the condition. In particular, we suggest that nonprofit hybridity should be understood as episodic insofar as it involves periods of "peace" and "war" among multiple organizing logics. Where organizational means and ends are clear and cohere with inhabitants' expectations of that type of organization and entity, logic peace will likely ensue. We see this clearly in the former CEO's term of office. Although the CEO was commercially minded and money-making was a core component of organizational life, it was only ever "oxygen" to enable the association to serve the profession and the public good. Doing the "right thing" in the "right way" mattered in the achievement of collective purposes. Where means and ends diverge with inhabitants' expectations and framing of organizational type and purpose, war is a likely outcome. Despite much effort to make the incumbent CEO's transformation of organizational purpose towards economic goals more palatable and inoffensive to internal audiences, the period was characterized by moral dilemmas, misuses of power and conflict. It was not just the (re)positioning of profit as the end game itself that proved problematic over time, but the idea that profit should be achieved "at any cost" – to employees, to trustees, to members, to the profession and to wider society. We would therefore argue that contestation in the negotiation and renegotiation of what are to be taken as organizational "means" and "ends" is central to understanding episodes of peace and war in hybrid organizing.

Our account also addresses institutional theory's "stubborn silence" on issues of social power (Greenwood et al., 2008, p.3; see also Meyer & Höllerer, 2014; Lok, 2019) and the "ideological structure of organizations" (Hinings & Greenwood, 2002, p. 415). Through our analysis of organizational change, as it unfolds *in situ* and over time, we shed significant light on the micro-processes and ideological foundations of institutional work in contexts of hybrid organizing. We did not find that managers (re)organize tasks and (re)structure organizations in a neutral and apolitical way to balance competing logics, as implied by much of the literature on strategic responses to hybridity discussed in Chapter 2. Rather, we found that "symbolic violence" (Boudieu & Passeron, 1990; Bourdieu & Wacquant, 1992) can permeate the institutional work undertaken to "encourage" others to identify with and then adopt practices congruent with managers' proffered logics. This occurs not least through naturalizing the (uneven) distribution of power, privilege and inequality to legitimate existing or create new structures of domination within organizations; the battle between and tactics employed by Mariella and Geoff in Chapter 3 is a case in point.

Practically, our account warns those involved in the governance of nonprofits in particular, that it is not enough to rely on the formalities of organizational life (e.g. development and oversight of appropriate policies and procedures or compliance with regulatory demands) to prevent malfeasance or malpractice. In our view, more regulation is not the answer. We have clearly shown that such measures can be circumvented through the informalities of organizational life, involving trade-offs, covert deals and secret bargains, the wholesale bypassing and/or mediation of formal, collective decision-making. Both the official rules of the game, and the informal aspects of organizational life, become entangled with each other in a (more or less) negotiated order. This points to the importance of developing a culture of social relations that serves to mediate and deliberate the (mis)use of power and authority. Within the pages of this book, we have exposed many signals that may indicate a loss of (social) purpose in nonprofits; we hope they serve as a source of vigilance to those who govern, manage, work and volunteer within them.

While we make no attempt in concluding our story to prescribe a blueprint for how organizing should be "done" in hybrid contexts, we leave you with a set of questions thrown up by our analysis of the association. They are based on the premise that sound governance and management has a moral and not just legal basis, and are intended to encourage interrogation of your own positionality in relation to such activities – or the study thereof – and how this may influence and bias your understanding and outlook on organizational life:

- What (conscious/subconscious) organizing principles (or logics) are you and others bringing to bare on nonprofit work organizations? What is desirable? How does this sit with commonly understood expectations of such organizations? To what extent are such matters explicitly foregrounded in (organizational and research) conversations?
- How do different individuals and groups of organizational inhabitants frame the organization's purpose and to what degree of consensus/divergence?
- How clearly delineated and deliberated are organizational means and ends among organizational inhabitants? What degree of conflict exists between the two and with what consequences?
- What degree of congruence exists between performance or "success" measures, individual reward and recognition systems, and the organization's raison d'être or purpose?
- What attitudes and behaviors are governance and management structures, systems and processes intentionally and/or unintentionally cueing to organizational inhabitants (trustees, staff, volunteers) and with what potential consequences?
- Where are governance conversations focused – Compliance? Policy? Social relations? Mission/purpose? What is being silenced in these conversations, by whom, why and at what cost?
- To what extent does the duration of trustee tenure-ships, and its interplay with organizational strategy cycles, afford the board a long-term view of organizational change or (intended/unintended) transformations of organizational trajectory?
- What formal and informal mechanisms are in place to identify, expose and address misuse of managerial power and authority? Are social relations between board members and employees/volunteers such that the latter trust board members would "do the right thing" in response to any (founded) disclosures?
- To what extent might you be "walking the corridors of compromise" in your current engagement with nonprofit work and organization?

References

Bain, C. (2017). *Interplay of Intentions: An Ethnography of Institutional Work Within a Hybrid Organization.* Unpublished DBA (Doctoral) Thesis. Sheffield, UK: Sheffield Hallam University.

Battilana, J., & Dorado, S. (2010). Building sustainable hybrid organisations: The case of commercial microfinance organisations. *Academy of Management Journal*, *53*(6), 1419–1440.

Boudieu, P., & Passeron, J. C. (1990). In R. Nice (Trans.), *Reproduction in Education, Society, and Culture*. London: Sage.

Bourdieu, P., & Wacquant, L. J. (1992). *An Invitation to Reflexive Sociology*. Chicago, IL: University of Chicago Press.

Currie, G., Lockett, A., Finn, R., Martin, G., & Waring, J. (2012). Institutional work to maintain professional power: recreating the model of medical professionalism. *Organization Studies*, *33*(7), 937–962.

Coburn, C. E. (2004). Beyond decoupling: rethinking the relationship between institutional environment and the classroom. *Sociology of Education*, *77*(3), 211–244.

Donaldson, L., & Davis, J. H. (1991). Agency theory and stewardship theory: CEO governance and shareholder returns. *Australian Journal of Management*, *16*, 49–64.

Duska, Ronald F. (September 1997). The why's of business revisited. *Journal of Business Ethics*, *16*(12/13), 1401–1409.

Duska, Ronald F. (2007). *Contemporary Reflections on Business Ethics*. Dordrecht: Springer.

Ericsson, D., & Kostera, M. (2020). Alterethnography: Reading and writing otherness in organizations. *Gender, Work and Organization*, *27*(6), 1–16. DOI: 10.1111/gwao.12503.

Friedman, M. (1970). *The social responsibility of business is to increase its profits. The New York Times Magazine*, 122–126, September 13, 1970.

Gawer, A., & Phillips, N. (2013). Institutional work as logic shift: The case of Intel's transformation to platform leader. *Organizational Studies*, *34*(8), 1035–1071.

Gomez, P. Y., & Korine, H. (2008). *Entrepreneurs and Democracy: A Political Theory of Corporate Governance*. Cambridge, MA: Cambridge University Press.

Green, S. A., Yuan, L., & Nohria, N. (2009). Suspended in self-spun webs of significance: a rhetorical model of institutionalization and institutionally embedded agency. *Academy of Management Journal*, *52*(1), 11–36.

Greenwood, R., Oliver, C., Sahlin, K., & Suddaby, R. (2008). Introduction. In R. Greenwood, C. Oliver, K. Sahlin & R. Suddaby (Eds), *The SAGE Handbook of Organizational Institutionalism* (pp. 1–46). London: Sage.

Haveman, H. A., & Rao, H. (2006). Hybrid forms and the evolution of thrifts. *American Behavioural Scientist*, *49*(7), 974–986.

Hinings, C. R., & Greenwood, R. (2002). Disconnects and consequences in organization theory? *Administrative Science Quarterly*, *47*, 411–421.

Höpfl, H. (2007). The codex, the codicil, and the codpiece: Some thoughts on diminution and elaboration on identity formation. *Gender, Work and Organization*, *14*(6), 619–632.

Jay, J. (2013). Navigating paradox as a mechanism of change and innovation in hybrid organisations. *Academy of Management Journal*, *58*(1), 137–159.

Klein, N. (2007). *The Shock Doctrine: The Rise of Disaster Capitalism*. Canada: Knopf.

Lawrence, T. B., & Suddaby, R. (2006). Institutions and institutional work. In Clegg, S. R., Hardy, C., Lawrence, T. B., & Nord, W. R., *Sage Handbook of Organizational Studies* (2nd Edition, pp. 215–254). London: SAGE.

Lok, J. (2019). Why (and how) institutional theory can be critical: Addressing the challenge to institutional theory's critical turn. *Journal of Management Inquiry*, *28*(3), 335–349.

Mannay, D., & Morgan, M. (2015). Doing ethnography or applying qualitative techniques? Reflections from the waiting field. *Qualitative Research*, *15*(2), 166–182.

Meyer, R. E., & Höllerer, M. A. (2014). Does institutional theory need redirecting? *Journal of Management Studies*, *51*(7), 1221–1233.

Mongelli, L., Rullani, F., Ramus, T., & Rimac, T. (2019). The bright side of hybridity: Exploring how social enterprises manage and leverage their hybrid nature. *Journal of Business Ethics*, *159*(2), 301–305.

Pache, A. C., & Santos, F. (2010). When worlds collide: The internal dynamics of organizational responses to conflicting institutional demands. *Academy of Management Review*, *35*(2), 455–476.

Pache, A., & Santos, F. (2013). Inside the hybrid organization: selective coupling as a response to competing institutional logics. *Academy of Management Journal*, *56*(4). 972–1001.

Powell, W. W., & Colyvas, J. A. (2008). Microfoundations of institutional theory. In *The Sage Handbook of Organizational Institutionalism* (pp. 276–288). London: SAGE.

Pullen, A., & Rhodes, C. (2008). Dirty writing. *Culture and Organization*, *14*(3), 241–259.

Skelcher, C., & Smith, S. R. (2015). Theorizng hybridity: Institutional logics, complex organisations, and actor identities in the case of nonprofits. *Public Administration*, *93*(2), 433–448.

Turco, C. (2012). Difficult decoupling: employee resistence to the commercialization of personal settings. *American Journal of Sociology*, *118*(2), 380–419.

Appendix – Detailed Account of Methods

We accounted for the ethnographic approach underpinning our tale of the association in Chapter 1 and provided modest details on methods. For those interested in a more detailed understanding, we delve further into the methods of data collection and analysis here.

Data collection occurred in two distinct but interrelated phases, summarized in Figure A1.1, and both involving document analysis, interviews and extensive observation. The first phase focused on the research context and if and how organizational inhabitants experienced and made sense of different organizing logics within the association. The second phase focused on incidents that appeared to have potential to shed light on the substantive questions guiding the overall research program.

A total of 26 in-depth interviews (or purposeful conversations) were undertaken, recorded and transcribed. A field journal was kept and updated regularly to include my reflections (musings) and observations. Documents, or written texts, were useful in exploring the construction of formal or official stories and shared narratives about individuals and the organization over time. Table A1.1 provides an overview of the various

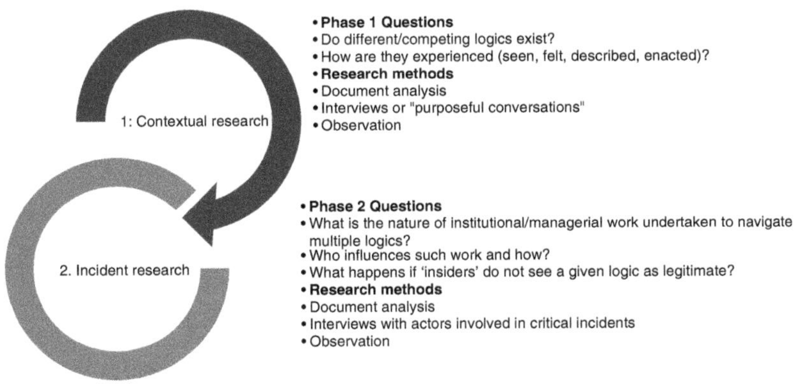

Figure A1.1 Research phases, questions and methods.

Table A1.1 Summary of data sources

Phase	*Title*	*Individual interviews/ purposeful conversations*	*Documents*		*Participant observation*
	Total	26 interviews with 19 individuals [350 interview transcript pages]	98 documents [2,566 document pages]		Attendance at 25 meetings as participant observer
1	Making sense of hybridity	14 [251 pages of interview transcript]	1374 pages	Strategy documents; Website pages; Charter document; Appraisal documents; Trustee meeting minutes; Senior executive meeting minutes; Staff away day films and presentation; Project and budget documents, Reflective log	• Trustee strategy setting meetings • Senior executive meetings • Functional team meetings (finance, governance and sales)
2	Incident 1: Data sharing	6 [118 pages of interview transcript]	114 pages	Job descriptions; Key performance indicators; ICT data flow document; Project document (P&L scoping Nov 14); Training handouts; Reflective log	• Monthly senior executive meeting • Training presentation/ workshop

Table A1.1 (Continued)

Phase	*Title*	*Individual interviews/ purposeful conversations*	*Documents*		*Participant observation*
	Incident 2: The bonus setting process	1 [27 pages of interview transcript]	500 pages	Job descriptions; Regulations/terms of reference; Email; Meeting reports; Great citations; Pay policy; Meeting minutes; Staff away day films and presentation; Reflective log	• Finance committees • Trustee meetings
	Incident 3: The governance setting	5 [102 pages]	578 pages	Job descriptions; Regulations/terms of reference; Email; Trustee meeting minutes; Reflective log	• Trustee meetings • Senior executive meetings

Source: Bain, 2017.

data sources before they are discussed in detail in relation to the two research phases.

Phase 1 – Making Sense of a Hybrid Context

The first phase of research was about how individuals and groups experienced and made sense of the association and its purpose. Specifically, I was looking to understand whether different purposes and organizing logics were articulated and, if so, how they were seen, felt, described, enacted and navigated. This initial phase consisted of fourteen audio-recorded and transcribed interviews, lasting approximately one hour each, with: two trustees; one current and one previous CEO; three senior managers (Directors), three middle managers; three (non-management) staff and one graduate. In total, there were 251 pages of interview transcripts. Participants were chosen for pragmatic reasons (ease of access) and to get a breadth and variation of experience amongst interviewees (See Table A1.2 for profile of interviewees in Phase 1). Specifically, I was looking to get perspectives from across the different areas of activity, job seniority and length of employment with the association.

In the interviews, participants were asked to share their own perspectives and experiences, beginning with their interpretation of the core purpose of the organization and their role within this. Interviews were loosely structured and conversational in style, allowing participants to pursue topics they felt were interesting and important rather than merely responding to researcher-determined parameters. The general topics included in the aid memoir that acted as a loose guide during interviews were evolved throughout the process through additional foci including how work is prioritized and success measured. Interviews were recorded and transcribed with copies provided to each participant for review, clarification, addendum, etc. Following each interview, I supplemented the material in my reflective log through recording my own observation and experience of the process. I also observed two functional team meetings in Phase 1 (finance and governance team and sales team) to get an appreciation of the issues that they were dealing with and the types of language they used/conversations they had. I read three strategy documents covering a nine-year period to see what issues were being dealt with, how the organization was being positioned, what the key priorities were and what constituted success within the formal or official articulation of the association. I undertook a physical environment scan, walking around the offices looking at the physical set-up, in addition to any symbolic messaging around the building to understand what key messages were conditioning our understanding of the organization. I referred to minutes of previous meetings I had attended, copies of my own annual appraisals and other institutional documents that I had gathered within the context of my role. I acted as participant observer in meetings that took place throughout my study that included Board meetings (trustees plus CEO); management meetings; meetings of the member representational group and functional team meetings (see Table A1.2 for details).

Remaining a "conscious researcher" at meetings was challenging at times, as I was often acting as a routine participant, forming relationships and participating in activities while at the same time making no secret of my intention to observe events as an ethnographer. In doing this I considered my own experiences as an important and legitimate source of data, incorporating auto-ethnographical aspects into data collection and analysis. To mitigate against a lapse of research attention (privileging participation rather than observation), I systematically recorded data through a mixture of reflective note taking on descriptions of people, events and conversations as well as recording and transcribing the recordings where possible. For more formal meetings I could use the formal minutes of the meeting to supplement observational data, while always being mindful that minutes are themselves a political artefact and shaped by individual sensemaking of the meeting conversation. Respectful of the need to be able to approach the data from multiple possible interpretations, the process of reflexivity was an essential feature of the research and Tracey played a crucial role here (see Preface to the book).

Initial analysis involved repeated engagement with interview recordings, transcripts, documents and my reflective log. As I did so, I noticed what seemed to be several phrases that individuals used to position the association. This invoked the notion of a "living conversation" where conversation among people is seen as a never-ending process whereby one person's message and meaning joins with that of another but to form a rather different "frame." In this way, I began to build the schematic of the different ways people position the organization and the logics that underpin these positions through an iterative process of reading and re-reading different data sources. The analytical outcomes of Phase 1 are seen most clearly in Chapter 2 of the book, *An Organization in Search of Purpose,* where we explore the multiple ways organizational inhabitants frame and make sense of the association and its purpose, and negotiate what are taken to be organizational means and ends. They also underpin elements of Chapters 3 *(Managers in Search of Purpose),* 4 *(Symbols, Rhetoric and Strategizing),* 5 *(Structuring for Purpose)* and 6 *(Rewarding Loyalty to the (New) Cause).* From this platform, my Phase 2 questions turned to the nature of institutional work undertaken to transform, promote and/or defend particular organizing logics, who influences such work and how and what happens if a given logic is not considered legitimate.

Table A1.2 Interviews – Phase 1

Role Level			*Relationship with focal organisation*					*Role description (by team position in organisation]*				
Senior	*Middle*	*Other*								*Commercial*	*Regulated*	*Services*
Strategic leader or trustee	Accountable for a function	Team leader, administrator or graduate placement	Volunteer	Previous employee now retired	Employed	Consultant	Years in role	Trustee	CEO	Responsible for revenue and profit	Responsible for setting standards and/ or regulated by an external regulator	Cost centre providing services to organisation such as finance/ HR/governance
1			1				5	1				
1			1				2	1				
1					1		6		1			
1				1			10		1			
1					1		8			1		
	1				1		2			1		
		1			1		3			1		
1					1		10				1	
		1				1	5				1	
1					1		23					1
	1					1	6					1
	1				1		5					1
		1			1		3				1	
		1			1		3					1
7	3	4	2	1	9	2	91	2	2	3	3	4

Source: Bain (2017)

Phase 2 – Incidents (of Logic War)

Phase 2 involved the identification and analysis of incidents that generated conflict within the association because of apparent contestation over contradictory organizing logics. My interest was in exploring the causes of the conflict, the institutional/managerial work that occurred to transform, defend, repair and/or legitimize logics and how this was received and responded to by various internal audiences. It is important to note that I did not undertake the traditionally positivistic approach of critical incident technique, but rather used "critical incidents" as the mechanism to guide the focus of ethnographic data collection. This was helpful in placing purposeful boundaries around the fieldwork within an embedded, longitudinal ethnography where literally everything and everyone could become the focus of an ethnographer's attention. In identifying what seemed to be a "critical" incident, rather than just another incident, I observed the level and significance of "noise" or "turbulence" created within the organization (i.e. how much and what kind of attention did the incident receive, from whom, for how long and why). Phase 2 revolved around three "events" or "incidents" in the field that are summarized in Table A1.3 below.

At this point, it is important to again acknowledge the role of my "insider" status in the identification of incidents. As a Director in the association, I had privileged access to certain types of conversation due to my leadership role and my functional remit (HR, IT, Procurement, Strategic Projects). My identification of incidents, and their potential significance, was undoubtably shaped by a combination of my developing theoretical knowledge and experiential "gut instinct" as a manager. Talking the selection of incidents through with Tracey as an "outsider" provided a useful counterbalance to my own closeness to them.

Incident 1 – Data Sharing

Fieldwork relating to Incident 1 consisted of three interviews, lasting approximately two hours each with two senior managers and a consultant involved in a specific project. In the interviews participants were asked to share their perspectives on and experiences of the incident and how they made sense of the issues involved. Additionally, I revisited three Phase 1 interviews where interviewees had referred to the incident in order to get an appreciation of how those who were not directly involved accounted for it. Again, I brought to the process my own experiences as an organizational inhabitant. For example, in my time with the association I had been responsible for the Information Technology (IT) team (so was familiar with the data sharing policies and data protection regulations) and for the operational activity that raised the

Table A1.3 Summary of incidents

Title of incident	*Summary of incident*	*How incident was identified*	*Incident data featured in.*
Data sharing	Involved one department (and Director) challenging another regarding an "un-authorized" marketing email and in doing so restricted data were accessed in an unfair way, putting the association at risk of a regulatory breach due to conflict of interest.	In my everyday work, I became aware of emotionally charged conversations between three departments (one alleging misuse of data/conflict of interest; one being accused of misuse of data and one trying to mediate between the two).	Chapter 3 – *Managers in Search of Purpose.*
The bonus setting process	Involved long-term changes to the bonus structure and wider pay and reward system that became increasingly contested at senior levels.	In my role, I was directly involved in the development of proposals and attending meetings to gain approval.	Chapter 4 – *Symbols, Rhetoric and Strategizing.* Chapter 6 – *Rewarding Loyalty to the (New) Cause.* Chapter 7 – *Immobilizing Resistance and Overcoming Dissent.*

The governance setting	Involved the Board of Trustees challenging the legality, authority and process of another group involved in the association's governance. Emphasis then evolved into other areas that challenged other aspects of governance such as CEO–Trustee duality.	I attended several meetings where I became aware of a narrative of challenge around a specific committee, which then started to diverge into other areas of governance.It came to my attention due to the longevity and increasing intensity of the contestation among senior individuals and groups.	Chapter 5 – *Structuring for Purpose.* Chapter 7 – *Immobilizing Resistance and Overcoming Dissent.* Chapter 8 – *Leading Away from Purpose and Getting Away with It.*

Source: Adapted from Bain (2017).

allegation of data misuse/conflict of interest (so was familiar with the regulatory framework). Furthermore, as a colleague of the two Directors concerned, and having worked directly with them for more than 5 years, I had my own relationship with them and brought to the discussion my experiences of their characters and motivations alongside knowledge of their individual roles and relationships with the other parties involved.

As with the interviews in Phase 1, participant identities were anonymized (through use of pseudonyms), interviews recorded and transcribed. Participants were provided with transcripts of their interview, after which I completed a reflective log, recording my initial interpretations about what was going on for the protagonist and reflections on the conversation. Finally, I provided a copy of my interpretations to three members of the internal reviewer group and invited their feedback on my interpretations and the extent to which it made sense and appeared credible to them, thus contributing to the reliability and authenticity of knowledge claims.

Incident 2 – The Bonus Setting Process

This incident was of a more confidential, sensitive nature in that the context of the incident (approving a new bonus) was one with the potential to affect the terms and conditions of staff employment. I was closely involved with the events as they unfolded as, at the time, my job role included responsibility for Human Resources (HR) and I line managed the HR team. This allowed for direct observation and involvement in conversations and processes "in situ." As such the sources of data for this incident were: organizational documents in the form of minutes of meetings, drafts of formal papers, nominations for bonus award over an extended time period; observational field notes of committee meetings and a reflective diary. Again, I provided early drafts to the reviewer group asking if "it made sense to them" and was a credible, authentic representation. Importantly due to the sensitivity of the subject matter, I did so only after the approval process was completed and the outcome had been communicated to all staff.

What struck me most about this incident was the strength of individuals' positions on an issue and that, on this occasion, there appeared to be two opposing "logics" towards a bonus scheme. The first view reflected a belief in "economic man" with its assumption that human behaviour is driven by financial reward. As such, the status of a bonus scheme was important, the focus was on maximizing the value of the bonus and the success measures were purely financial – somewhat odd in the context of a charity/Royal Charter organization legally bound to "Public Good." The alternative view positioned the bonus as a "nice to have," a means of showing what matters in terms of means as well as (multiple) ends. As such, a modest bonus was a way of signaling what mattered and a way to say thank you to staff.

Incident 3 – The Governance Setting

This incident was of a political (distribution of power) and regulatory nature and one that caused a good deal of frustration and conflict among elite actors. The data sources consisted of four (recorded and transcribed) interviews, lasting between one and two hours with one Trustee and three Senior Managers/Directors. Two of the Senior Managers had more than twenty years' service each within the association. My initial interview questions were positioned around the current structure of governance and how interviewees made sense of the changing governance structure. From this, other questions emerged regarding the work undertaken by specific individuals in relation to structural changes and what challenges they faced in bringing about change. Additionally, I returned to the transcript of one interview in Phase 1, where a colleague referred to governance structures and processes within the association.

Additionally, my insider status led me to observing (and participating) in eight trustee board meetings over a two-year period. At the end of each meeting I recorded my reflections, thoughts and feelings in my research diary/reflective log, which were used as part of my reflexive and interpretation process and in discussion with Tracey. Trustee meetings were supported by documentation (such as presentations, minutes, draft proposals for changes to terms of reference) that related to the structural changes proposed and undertaken, and the discussions relating to them that I used in conjunction with the interviews and my log. As I listened to the tapes and reviewed the transcripts, documents and journal notes, what struck me most was the iterative changes made to structure over time – almost as if by making small incremental changes, the CEO was reducing the risk of challenge and making changes by stealth. Rather ironically, the "professionalization" rationale for the changes – that were intended to result in more autonomy for the CEO – actually resulted in the recruitment of powerful, agentic actors who directly challenged the ideology that brought them to the association in the first place.

As with the Phase 1 analysis, the first step in analyzing the incident data was to repeatedly listen to the audio recordings, review documentation and reflective log entries. I drew free-hand sketches to develop visual mind maps of who was involved, what roles they played, what was occurring and how different aspects of the incidents related to other aspects of the same and other incidents. I then wrote an incident narrative, including a) a precis of the incident, b) the data that relate to it, c) identification of the protagonists, d) how the incident relates to the wider organizational environment, e) what happened from the protagonists' perspectives and f) a summary and theorization of my interpretation. From the individual incident mind maps and narratives, I noticed some recurring concepts and themes that were again mapped visually to aid theorization across the incidents and form the basis of our concluding chapter (Chapter 9).

As before, I read and re-read the documents and transcripts in an iterative manner, looking for surprises or unexpected data and at times cycling between the documents and the literature to refine and build analytical understanding. I sensechecked and refined my understanding through the group of people who reviewed chapters (and in conversations with Tracey and my supervisors), looking to ensure that my interpretation was received as authentic and credible, that it resonated and had meaningful congruence with the reviewer group. By way of concrete example, I conceptualized rhetorical work (discussed in Chapter 9) as a result of reading Turco (2012) who puts *euphemistic* discourses, or creating the appearance of inoffensive messages, at the heart of organizational change. Noticeable in the transcripts and documents was the use of this tactic by elite actors within their rhetorical work. I subsequently went back to the transcripts to see exactly how they were doing this and found three core processes: giving protection to an existing symbolic order to provide an underlying structure of meaning for participants; using a nestling strategy that embeds new ideas into the existing script to provide legitimacy; evolving the existing discourse to create a bridging narrative (see Chapter 9 for a full discussion). This process is depicted in Figure A1.2.

The re-interpretation and re-writing of the incidents into the constituent chapters of this book manuscript, led by Tracey, was subject to a similar process. It involved returning to mind maps, theorizing narratives and the incident data in order to move beyond the incidents to examine and elaborate what they tell us about different aspects of organizing

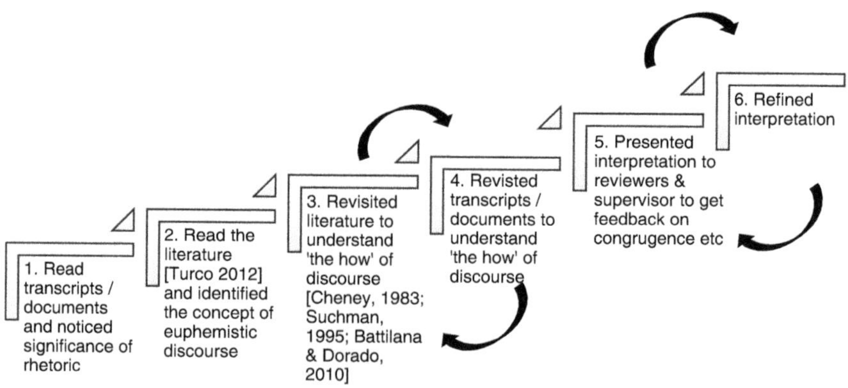

Figure A1.2 Illustrative sequence of analysis.

(strategy, governance, leadership and so on). The chapters then underwent introspective interrogation by me, from the vantage point of both senior manager and embedded ethnographer, and by a former colleague at the association. How the data from the incidents relate to the structure and content of this book is summarized in Table A1.3.

Our tale of the association represents what we consider to be the richest (and often most contentious) points of a longitudinal, embedded ethnography. It includes words and moments that appear to carry significance to those of us who inhabited the association in that period of time, interwoven with insights from the literature to theorize and highlight the often unspoken, soft underbelly of organizational life and managerial work in nonprofits.

About the Authors

Tracey's research focuses on two overlapping themes: the marginalization and prioritization of different forms and processes of nonprofit governance and organization and the social–political dynamics of state–nonprofit relations in welfare systems. She has served on the editorial board of *Voluntary Sector Review,* is Research-to-Practice Editor at *Nonprofit and Voluntary Sector Quarterly (NVSQ)* and has published in international journals such as *NVSQ*, *Public Administration* and *Business and Society*. She held research and policy analysis roles within the nonprofit and public sectors before entering academia.

Carole started her career as an Officer in the Royal Air Force, Secretarial Branch, then spent a significant period of time in an education charity setting, including over a decade in senior leadership roles. In 2017 she completed a professional doctorate (Doctorate in Business Administration) at Sheffield Hallam University. Her research focuses on sensemaking in hybrid organizations. She is an associate member of the Chartered Institute of Personnel Development and a fellow of the Chartered Management Institute.

Index

www.ingramcontent.com/pod-product-compliance
Ingram Content Group UK Ltd.
Pitfield, Milton Keynes, MK11 3LW, UK
UKHW022018180926
475701UK00005B/903
* 9 7 8 0 3 6 7 7 1 1 0 4 7 *